THE WEIL LECTURES ON AMERICAN CITIZENSHIP
OF THE UNIVERSITY OF NORTH CAROLINA

CITIZENSHIP TODAY

THE WEIL LECTURES ON AMERICAN CITIZENSHIP

IN PRINT:

JACOB H. HOLLANDER
American Citizenship and Economic Welfare

R. GOODWYN RHETT
The Progress of American Ideals

WILLIAM BENNETT MUNRO
Personality in Politics

FELIX FRANKFURTER
The Commerce Clause

HENRY A. WALLACE
Technology, Corporations, and the General Welfare

T. V. SMITH
Discipline for Democracy

GALO PLAZA
Problems of Democracy in Latin America

CARLOS P. ROMULO
The Meaning of Bandung

D. W. BROGAN
Citizenship Today

CHAPEL HILL: THE UNIVERSITY OF NORTH CAROLINA PRESS

CITIZENSHIP TODAY

England—France—The United States

BY

D. W. Brogan, F.B.A., LL.D.

*Fellow of Peterhouse and Professor of Political Science
in the University of Cambridge*

CHAPEL HILL

THE UNIVERSITY OF NORTH CAROLINA PRESS

PRINTED BY THE SEEMAN PRINTERY, DURHAM, N. C.

To Joan Chenhalls

PREFACE

WHEN THE UNIVERSITY of North Carolina did me the
great honor of inviting me to give the Weil Lectures,
it was suggested that "citizenship" would make an
appropriate and timely topic. I thought that the
topic could be most usefully treated, in the short com-
pass of three lectures, by my discussing what seemed
to me the more urgent problems of citizenship in three
countries which, if I do not know them well, I know
better than I know any others. I also thought it
might be profitable to concentrate, in the case of each
country, on one set of problems. I have therefore not
repeated in each lecture the enumeration of the problems that surround the theory and practice of citizenship in any modern society. Some problems I
have ignored altogether; others, like juvenile delin-
quency, I have briefly alluded to; others I have illustrated almost entirely from one country. I have
assumed a common body of democratic doctrine and
a smaller body of common democratic practice. I
have dwelt on the historical background, since one of
the problems facing these societies is the survival of
vigorous historical traditions that are not fully relevant to the present day. And if I have not stressed
it, I hope that the common truth will not be forgotten
that the peoples of England, France, and the United

States are members of a new society which has not yet found an adequate theory or an adequate practice of living together. In that, they are like all other human beings. Since these lectures were delivered, much has happened that might call for expansion if not alteration, especially in the field of French relations with Algeria and the Community. But nothing has happened to alter the general picture I attempted to give and I have avoided the temptations of hindsight.

D. W. Brogan

December, 1959

CONTENTS

CITIZENSHIP TODAY

CITIZENSHIP IN ENGLAND

IT IS PROPER to begin these lectures with some attempt at definition. We naturally take the concept of "citizenship" for granted; we are not much concerned, normally, with precision in the description of either rights or duties involved in the concept, we claim our rights, and we do some, even many, of our duties without any reflection. But it is well to stress, at the beginning, the notions I have of what the rights and duties of a citizen are, not only because that is academically decorous, but because in this age and this world, the traditional concept is under attack or, at the very best, is tampered with and travestied, to the bewilderment not only of newcomers to the concept of citizenship but of inheritors of the concept, who often seem to treasure it more than they understand what it implies.

The newcomers? Yes. For a great part of the world, the notion of citizenship is novel, has few roots in indigenous institutions, and calls for new habits of mind and behavior for which past social experience provides little preparation. We can only begin to understand our own inheritance, and what it gives and demands, if we begin by accepting the proposition that the concept of citizenship is not one universally given by human experience, if we accept the fact that great civilizations have got on without it, and if we accept as a possibility that the technological world creating a technically unified human society may be the enemy, not the friend, of the idea of citizenship.

It will be easier to make this last point if I return now to the problem of definition. A citizen is not merely a political or social animal. The innocent eighteenth-century idea of the noble savage, of the possibility of human existence and human rights outside organized society, need not detain us. We know that what we call, often with too much disdain, a "savage" society is an extremely complicated set of social obligations and social claims. It could be said that part of the progress of civilization up till recent times was the freeing of man in society from the exorbitant, all-embracing claims of society, progress "from status to contract," to quote Sir Henry Maine. Many of the phenomena that I shall discuss in these lectures have their counterparts in New Guinea or the Congo, had their counterparts in the cultures of Creeks and Iroquois.

But in these societies, the idea of citizenship is either absent or present in an extremely rudimentary form. What is this idea? It seems to me to have two aspects. The first—possibly the most important, certainly the most novel—aspect is the assumption that every citizen has the right to be consulted on the conduct of the political society and the duty of having something to contribute to the general consultation. The second aspect is the converse of the first. The citizen who has a right to be consulted is bound by

the results of the consultation.   His duties flow from
his rights.

In a primitive or, if you like, normal but non-
European society, the concept of duty is deeply im-
bedded.   These societies make and have made what
seem to us exorbitant claims on their members.   They
demand and get, or got, loyalty to the death.   Societies of this type have had long and brilliant lives.
They have answered one of the great problems of
political philosophy: how to get the members of that
society to prefer, at times, the good of the society (or
what is asserted to be its good) to the immediate
human desire to stay alive or not to starve.   But the
loyal service given to a society, usually but not always embodied in a single person—and that person
usually if not always believed to embody divine
authority—is not the embodiment of citizenship.   It
may produce the same material goods, wealth, order,
victory, the splendid worship of the God or gods, the
maintenance of the tribal tradition.   But these end
products, equalled in societies based on citizenship
though not necessarily surpassed in them, are not the
results of "good citizenship."   They are the results of
loyalty, of service, of something we may call even in
its primitive forms patriotism.   The social life that is
the ground and the result of these political habits may
support many or most civilized values.   But we are
committed to another concept, to another way of
creating the conditions for what we believe to be the
good life here on earth.   "Fear God and honor the
King" was an adequate political creed for early
Christians in an absolute state where the relics of a

state based on citizenship were merely relics. But it is not enough for us, although some of the trends of modern society may be gently preparing us for a day when we shall be content with a modern equivalent of the Pauline counsel and when the forms of a government by citizens will conceal but not alter the realities of government by technocrats.

The basic difference lies in the Western rejection of the assumption that the will of the king or chief is law, is absolute, is to be obeyed without question (although an extremity of cruelty, aggression, or incompetence may provoke revolt). Respect is due to the traditions of the people and still more to its God or gods, but the right of the king is to command, the duty of the people is to obey. Such was the monarchy in China, in India, and in Israel. There can be Solomon; there can be Ahab. There can be wise ministers like Joseph and brave prophets like Nathan, but there is no place for the citizen.

In a society based on citizenship, the ruler, rather, the holder of political office, not only expounds the law and enforces it but is visibly and immediately subject to it. He is surrounded, if political authority is embodied in one man, by councillors not all of whom are arbitrarily chosen by him, councillors with their own irreducible minimum of rights and duties who in turn are chosen by or must win, not merely command, the "will of the people," "the citizens." And these citizens have not only the right to be consulted but the duty to give counsel. They are part of, not under, the governing body. In obeying the laws and the officers of the laws, they are obeying something they have inherited, something they own, something they have chosen.

I have neither the time nor the knowledge to develop this theme further. I am aware of some of the objections that can be made to my too brief, too schematic exposition. I am aware that it is possible to argue that the Aztec state of Montezuma's time was really a republic. I am aware that there were and are genuine consultation and some of the rights and duties of citizenship in the villages of India. I am aware that in some so-called republics, the great majority of the inhabitants were not citizens, in ancient Sparta and in eighteenth-century Poland, for instance. But there *were* citizens in Sparta and in Poland and there were none, in my sense, in ancient Persia or in Manchu China.

I think it is worthwhile to stress this point, for what we are to consider in these lectures is the present position of the citizen and the duties and rights of citizenship in three political societies which do in fact draw their ideas of citizenship (including their acceptance of the ideal of citizenship) from a common ancestry, that of the Graeco-Roman city state modified by Hebraeo-Christian ethical biases or dogmas. It is this idea of citizenship that is loose in the world today, so powerful that it is imitated—and counterfeited—in societies where the idea has no deep historical roots, and it is this idea of citizenship that is threatened, questioned, more in practice than as yet in theory, in the three nations I propose to discuss.

Before I move on to that discussion, I should like to affirm my belief that many of the problems are common to all human societies that have entered the new technological world—and all human societies have done that or are doing it. But we are concerned with the Western world from which that concept comes and where it has known its greatest success and has found its most complicated form. The whole world is now moving into the orbit of our culture and it uses, abuses, understands, and misunderstands our ideas; this, if it is a matter of pride, is also a matter of deep responsibility.

It is my belief that in practical discussions (such as I hope this is), example tells better than verbal definition. And I turn from the assertion of the unique Western character of the idea of citizenship, of the combination of rights and duties based on mutual consent of the members of a political society, to its exemplification in the past and present state of England. First of all, I must justify my use of the word "England" in this country where the words "Britain" and "British" have nearly driven out the older terms "England" and "English." I do not deny—with my Irish and Scottish background it would be absurd to deny—that it is often useful to say "British" instead of "English." But it is often misleading, too. For what I am concerned with is a historical phenomenon of great importance of a markedly individual character which is English in its origins, not British, and has remained English even since the creation of a British state in 1707. And it is perhaps not necessary to underline the fact that despite the great contribution of Scotch, Irish, and Scotch-Irish, jointly and severally, to the history of

North Carolina, most of your political, legal, and social institutions are English in origin. When I mean British, I shall say British, but the social and political system that I wish to describe is that of the English state.

A second point, not altogether trivial but not as serious as the first (where the use of the wrong adjective may provoke the "praefervidum ingenium Scotorum"), is the ambiguity of the word "citizen" as applied to a member of the British body politic. Legally, I am not a citizen but a subject. Or, rather, I am both, for if I am a subject at home, I am, so my passport tells me, a British citizen abroad. But the normal and ancient and respectable term is "subject." And that fact underlines something important about the character of citizenship in England. It is a status based not so much on a general doctrine of the relation of the member of a political society to the government as on a series of claims made over a long historical period against a government based on indefeasible rights given by divine authority, by the right of conquest, or by a vague and undefined "law of the land," to a hereditary monarch. Again, to indulge in what I hope will be judged to be necessary historical shorthand, the rights of the subject and of the citizen have accumulated over centuries; they have not been defined and asserted in a body of doctrine at one time. It has been a matter, as Tennyson put it complacently but not unjustly, of "Freedom slowly broadening down from precedent to precedent." I am aware that this is too simple a story. I am aware that there were general theories of the rights and duties of kings in the Middle Ages, that the English king was never anything like an absolute monarch, even when he had ceased to be a tribal chief or was undoubtedly a conqueror or the heir of a conqueror. I am aware that England was part of Christendom so that she shared with France, Italy, Germany, and other Christian lands political institutions and principles that allowed for a high degree of consent among the subjects of Christian kings and indeed organized various violent and semiviolent ways of dissent. No medieval monarch could say, like a Chinese emperor, "tremble and obey." And if lawyers asserted in the famous Latin formula that "the will of the prince has the force of law," they also cited more republican maxims. But it is worth noting that for various reasons, mainly geographical, England had a different and privileged history and that, very early made a unified state, she was one marked by the imprint of her own peculiar legal system. Not all of these things were an advantage. Many obsolete institutions survived to work mischief. England, smug in her own ways, escaped the beneficial effects of having her legal system refreshed by Roman law, a refreshment that produced the best legal system in the world in her neighbor, Scotland. But whatever the balance of advantage (and I am convinced that it was on the English side), the English idea of citizenship has been and in many ways still is an idea of a not necessarily symmetrical system of rights and duties that is the birthright of the Englishman or, as Milton complacently put it, of "God's Englishman." (It is a foreign illusion that the English think God is an Englishman; they merely know that He has chosen and approves of them—as indeed they know that He should.)

And to avoid the lively and vigilant critics that any academic audience provides, I remind you and myself that a great deal of very bad history has gone into the creation of the English idea of the citizen. I know that the Magna Carta of the seventeenth-century lawyers is not the Magna Carta of King John or of Cardinal Langton or still less of the barons of Runnymede. I know that King Alfred did not establish trial by jury nor Simon de Montfort create, full-blown, the House of Commons. But these legends, false as they are in fact and certainly in emphasis, are important in that they have bred in the English mind a prejudice in favor of an institution because it is there, because it is old. Its beneficent qualities may have been worn away by time or occulted by craft or let lapse by neglect, but you can always—or you could always—go back to the good old laws of the good old times. Freedom was not a thing in the future but a thing once possessed by all Englishmen, if occasionally lost or diminished. The rights of the subject could never be lost merely by lapse. If the legal maxim had it that time could not run against the rights of the crown, the political maxim was equally insistent that time could not run against the rights of Englishmen. And if the Englishman was called a subject, not a citizen, that did not make him in his own eyes less secure in his rights and dignity or less ready to do the duty that flowed from those rights and that dignity. As much as Pericles or St. Paul, he

could boast that he was a citizen of no mean city—
even if his expression of the status was feudal, not
republican, in form.

It is possible to suggest that there was a dark side,
that there is a dark side, to this complacent inheritance of rights and duties. It is not only that old
institutions may survive their usefulness, that a whole
series of good customs may corrupt a state. It is not
only that traditional duties may cease to be relevant
and not be replaced by others more necessary for the
good of the kingdom and the subject. It is even possible to doubt if the history of England is one great
success story. It is possible to draw up a balance
sheet showing a high price being charged for both
"progress" and the preservation of old rights. The
Reformation had a high price; so had the overthrow
of the old feudal monarchy under Charles I—and the
prevention of the creation of a new, efficient monarchy. So had the failure of Cromwell to create an
efficient, modern, middle-class state. But such book-
keeping is irrelevant to my theme except when it casts
a light on some problems of contemporary England,
when the habits and institutions of the seventeenth
century may turn out to be a nuisance today. What
we have to accept is that in England, historical habit,
more than legal or political doctrine, conditions the
practice of citizenship, explains the claims made and
not made, the duties accepted and not accepted.
When I come to France and the United States I shall
have to deal with countries in which, no doubt, habit
plays a great part. Habit keeps society together in
every stage of history. But in England habit is

consciously more sacred than it is in either the United States or France, and there is in the national temper a great deal of that conservatism, described in the maxim of academic politics laid down, ironically, by F. M. Cornford: "Nothing should ever be done for the first time." So things continue to be done because they were done; things are not done because they were not done. Or, to be more accurate, the fact that things are not being done, even if they were done for centuries, the fact that something new is being done —these evasions of national conservatism are concealed from the Englishman. He wishes them to be concealed; and it is not too paradoxical to say that you can do anything new in England, even things extravagantly novel, if you pretend that really something very like this was done under Ethelred the Unready. Perhaps this pageant which barely conceals the realities deceives no one but American tourists, but that the pageant should still go on tells us a good deal about the English attitude (not the Scottish, not the Irish) to the problem of adjusting the national life, the rights and duties of subjects, to the age of the H bomb.

Are there any practical consequences, other than the multiplication of machinery, the addition of real to formal offices, that flow from the traditional character of English citizenship? There is one that will not be a novelty to Americans but is a novelty to French citizens, who find the practice, if not the theory, hard to digest. That is the survival into our times of the medieval institution of the privileged corporation affected, to use a more modern term, with a public character and so liable to public regulation, but normally autonomous, normally doing its own business in its own way and offering privileges to and imposing duties on its members in a way that a rigorous jurist might say involved a delegation from the sovereign power, but which the man in the street would rightly see simply as a corporate body of Englishmen exercising rights that, maybe, they got in the past from the crown but now hold by something like indefeasible right of possession. Besides the legal corporations of this type (of which the Oxford and Cambridge colleges are the instances that naturally come to my mind), there are the thousands of societies for all kinds of purposes that embody, for their purpose, a group of subjects who, for that purpose, act as citizens who have a right to create their own bodies politic.

It is not merely that they have a right; they have a duty to form such societies. The Englishman who is not a member of any society, who does not subscribe to any society, who has no ideas or wishes at all in the field of the maintenance of old rights or the conquest of new ones, is not a true-born Englishman; he is displaying an indifference to his duty as a subject (or citizen) that makes him, whether he votes or not, less than a full and deserving member of the commonwealth.

It should be noted that this tradition antedates the coming of universal suffrage for men, not to speak of women. Beneath and beside the limited body politic, in the narrow sense, were the innumerable societies, the dissenting churches, and, even in the eighteenth century, the London mob. The peasant or the town worker who joined a Methodist meeting or a radical society or even took part in a riot for "Wilkes and Liberty" was exercising his right and doing his duty. He might have no voice in the choice of members of the House of Commons, but he was learning and handing down what he had learned of the nature of citizenship.

It would be absurd to pretend that such societies, that such a training in citizenship, were confined to England. You can find equivalents or near equivalents in the Roman and Chinese empires. There were Christian burial societies (they built the catacombs); there were secret societies (they were and perhaps are a headache to Chinese governments of very different types). In medieval and post-medieval Europe there were hundreds of such societies in every state. Alone among the great states, England kept and rejuvenated the medieval concept of the autonomous society, and those societies stepped in where the English state refused to tread. For (and it is a great difference that puts American society on one side with English habit and puts French society on another with German, Italian, and Russian), the English state, if it freely called on its subjects to carry out many of the functions of the state for nothing, also refused to do many things that by the beginning of the modern age in the eighteenth century were already visibly necessary. And so we have private police forces, private fire brigades, bridge companies, turnpike companies, hospitals, schools, great economic institutions like Lloyds or the London Clearing

House, growing up in the midst of medieval survivals
like the City of London or the Oxford colleges, beside
new chartered institutions like the Bank of England,
the Royal Society, the Royal Academy. When a
need arose, it was assumed, often but not always
rightly, that a private group of citizens would meet
the need, that the state could and should wait until it
was manifest that the need was not being met before
it acted. That often meant a generation or two of
muddle, dirt, and neglect. Again, we are not concerned with drawing up a balance sheet but with
stressing the truth that, for the average Englishman,
the duties of citizenship, at any rate until very
modern times, involved doing many things in collaboration with private citizens, possibly with the
express permission of the state, possibly without it,
possibly against the will of the state. Nevertheless,
the duties and rights of the subject were never exhausted by his political rights and duties, even if we
extend those rights and duties to include the right and
duty of serving as a juryman or as a parish constable
or member of the *posse comitatus*. I shall try a little
later to show that these traditional ways of the
English polity are not adequate for today and have
ceased to be adequate for a generation past, at least.
But what I am here concerned to stress is the importance of the political education that the English
people received. They had rights and duties other
than those that the king imposed on some of them.
No man was incapable of, or excused from, the duties
of citizenship, and there was a continous chain of such
duties from the peasant or craftsman to the great

lord summoned to give counsel to the "King in Parliament." And it is one of the problems of today whether that chain of service, of duty or obligation, is still holding and how dangerously weak some of its links may be.*

But it is time to turn from the special historical character of the English state and of the English idea of citizenship and to examine its relevance and efficacy today. That it was a success can be admitted. It saved England from violent revolution; it did not inhibit progress. (The industrial revolution that has been gathering speed ever since and conquering the world was a British—not merely an English—achievement, beginning in the Glasgow of Professor Adam Smith and James Watt and in the Birmingham of Watt and Boulton. It produced the highest level of living in Europe and a degree of national unity triumphantly tested in the solitary, finest hour of 1940.)

But what of today? It is necessary to insist that long before the coming of the present welfare state, inadequacy of the old, strictly limited, amateur theory of government was visible. From the end of the great French war, critics like the Benthamites and others had been demanding that the state do more, although what they wanted was still very little by

* When I was an undergraduate at Balliol College, Oxford, a very hotly conducted by-election took place for the city's parliamentary seat. I returned to my rooms one morning and found there my elderly and dignified "scout" (servant), who asked me if I was taking any interest or any part in the election. I was in a hurry and replied, not quite truthfully, that I wasn't. He looked at me solemnly and said, "I believe, sir, that there were people in ancient Greece called idiots." I was properly rebuked.

French and still less by Prussian standards. But a regular police supplanted the old Dogberries; the old medieval units of local government were replaced by a more rational modern system. The state began to teach. It began to provide housing, pensions, some medical treatment. Possibly the main burden of the social services was still borne by private societies. There were private hospitals and a constellation of private schools from Eton to modern equivalents of Dotheboys Hall. Lifeboats run by a private society rescued ships insured at Lloyds. The Bank of England was a partly private corporation and the other banks were totally private corporations. Friendly societies organized relief from the catastrophies of life and even when the state entered the field, it shared, in the Act of 1911, responsibility with Oddfellows and Foresters.

But the trend was all one way. The camel had entered the tent. Perhaps it was of only historical interest that the grand jury, with so august a history, disappeared. But when the state, in the long depression that began in 1920 and did not end until the war of 1939, expanded the old idea of poor relief into an acceptance of the duty to meet such uncontrollable catastrophes as the turning of the terms of trade against Britain, the old idea of the adequacy of private charity was abandoned. The "dole," as it was scornfully called, was not lavish; its administration was rigorous. But the fact that a man on the dole was still allowed to vote, not marked off as being, by the fact of being on relief, unworthy to be a citizen, was significant of much.

Building societies still did their traditional work, but a higher and higher proportion of the population was housed by local authorities and subsidized by the central government or the local government or both. There was a central road fund, and for most activities local authorities depended on central subsidies for the necessary funds. And there was a consequent change in the idea of the rights and duties of a citizen. He could now vote to subsidize his own house. Unwillingly idle, he could protest by his vote against the inadequacy of aid given him. Then, more and more, the central and remote govenment decided how he and everybody else should be treated.

It was not only that a profound reorganization of local government areas in 1929 gave England a relevant system of local authorities, more relevant to modern conditions than that enjoyed by either France or the United States, but that it gave more and more powers to big authorities; it made the freedom of action of all local authorities conform to norms laid down in London. Cities and counties could not borrow without the permission of the central government. In education, in all forms of local administration, the view was implicitly expressed that "London knows best." For the citizen proud of his county, city, village, there was now the chilling thought that none of these units was really autonomous any longer and that to get a final answer to local questions he had to appeal to Caesar in faraway Whitehall.

An inevitable consequence of this change has been the mingling of local with national politics or, if you like, the supersession of local politics by national politics. The local government system created in the nineteenth century had only a nominal connection with the old medieval system. Names might survive. There is still a lord mayor of London, but for two generations past he has been far less important than the chairman of the London county council. The system set up over a century ago, and continually expanded since, had this in common with the old medieval order: it assumed that citizens would serve their own towns and counties without pay simply because it was their duty as well as their right. And serving in this way did not take up an exorbitant amount of time, except in case of the mayor of a borough or lord lieutenant of a county who might have to spend a good deal of money and a great deal of time in social functions. Limited in their field of action but nearly independent in what they did in the field, the local government units could call on local magnates, country gentlemen, businessmen, lawyers, bankers, retired army officers, on all the "natural" leaders of the hundreds of communities into which the country had been divided by history as well as by statute. It was not only that the rising tide of democratic sentiment resented the innocent claim to pre-eminence put forward by the "right people" but that the job became more and more onerous, more and more time-consuming.

Then the range of local government was increasingly determined by the temper of the central government, as well as by positive legislation by parliament and actual administration by "Whitehall." The parties, on the national scale, began to want to act on the local scale. Possibly it was the rise of the Labor party, challenging the middle- and upper-class oligarchy of the two old parties, the Conservatives and the Liberals, that forced party discipline on local authorities. Perhaps it was the inevitable result of the intrusion of the central government into local affairs. In any event, the change was made. In more and more city and county councils, party divisions followed national party alignments. This had a double result in changing the character of the citizen's duty and opportunities. He no longer had the chance of voting for men entirely on local issues. Occasionally, he could act the mugwump and refuse to vote the local ticket of the party to which, nationally, he adhered. In some cities, if not in many, this possibility of independent voting imposed decorum on the local party machine. But the cases were not numerous. Nor were the cases in which a local man, with local appeal, could ignore the national party labels and get elected on his own merits in a city otherwise dominated by one of the national parties. (Indeed, when he did this it might be under the label of "Liberal," since there was hardly any national Liberal party to impose any discipline.)

But a more serious result from the point of view of the decline in the active participation of public-spirited citizens in local politics was the sterility, in too many cases, of such participation. For if party discipline was strict (and it was more and more strict), the chance of independent action was slight.

If all issues were decided in the majority caucus, the chance of making an independent contribution, even if you were a member of the majority party, was small, and if you were a member of the minority party, it was nil. Can we wonder that local government attracts fewer and fewer people of independent views, of active careers, of energy and dignified ambition? The old training of electors—and elected—in local citizenship is much harder to come by today.

Then, the increase in the powers of the central government has eaten into the prestige and the interest of local government in another way. Many of the most important decisions are made in London. It is natural to use what political power you have or think you have where it will count most—not in the local town or county hall but in the House of Commons. So the local member of parliament is called on by his voters to make claims, to utter protests, to give advice in fields of government that are either only partly in the competence of the central government or still entirely in the competence of the local government. Yet it is often to the member of parliament that the voter goes, even if all that he can do is to refer the troubled political client to the appropriate local official or local councillor.

It would be unjust to end on a note of contempt or even boredom because local government is now so party-ridden as well as so rigorously controlled by the central government. English local government is in general honest. There are few perquisites and little graft. Government is efficient, if unenterprising, and local pride is far from being extinct. But local government only attracts attention when there is a scandal or a row. The English elector who does his duty by voting at national elections stays away in droves at local elections.

How can this decline in local interest, local service, local activity in citizenship, be remedied? Possibly a change in the electoral laws that would, by proportional representation, make it easier for minorities to get representation, that would lessen the chance of an automatic, overwhelming party superiority being established for good, would make service in the local authorities more attractive than it is at present, when party loyalty is more important than ability or energy. Possibly if the central government were less concerned to prevent local authorities from making mistakes and by law and administration allowed them more initiative, there might be a revival of local interest in local government and with it a revival of the education in citizenship that local government once provided. But it is hard to be optimistic, and one can only say in the face of public lethargy that Britain (I say Britain, for the case is as depressing in Scotland) gets a better local government than its politically lazy citizens deserve.

Politically lazy? Not in national politics. In national elections, the number of voters is always more than 80 per cent, and even in safe seats, where the minority party cannot win, there is a creditable turnout of the faithful few. Nor is it hard to get candidates for parliament. The Englishman is still, at any rate by American standards, a political animal. His vote is both a privilege and a duty. Often doggedly partisan (most people never change their party allegiance), unless we can assume that one party is always right—and we can't, obviously, assume that both are always right—it follows that millions of voters are incapable of responding to argument or changing conditions. Yet the voter who has decided that it is more important to vote for national than for local leadership shows in this age of peace and war, of the H bomb and of the control of the economy by the government, a proper sense of proportion. It may be a pity he pays so little attention to local politics, but if he has to choose he has chosen the better part.

Yet the forces that are sterilizing local government are at work in national politics, too. It is inevitable in London, as in Washington and Paris, that the executive, with its far greater range of information, its greater immediate responsibility, its inevitable near monopoly of the limelight, must have the better part in the political drama. The House of Commons, so ancient, so august, is only imperfectly the "grand inquest of the nation." (An unkind critic has suggested as an emendation to the old phrase, "in the Grand Inquest of the Nation, the House of Commons is the corpse.") But there is a special limitation on the power of the House of Commons to check, much more to rival, the executive, the "cabinet," the prime minister. The English governmental system which invented the modern party system sometime in the eighteenth century, at any rate not later than the first half of the nineteenth century, created an instrument of government that is in danger of killing its parent, parliament. For party discipline has now reached a height of perfection that would make the career of a Churchill impossible. It is not that there is no single member in the present House of Commons claiming to be an "independent." But there are few inside the two dominant parties who dare to be independent, to put their consciences above the party line, dare to live up to the proud premises of Burke's famous "Letter to the Sheriffs of Bristol," dare to give their voters their judgment, not their obedience. For the voters have been trained to expect of their members not judgment but docility to the orders of the party high command. No doubt party leaders listen to the complaints, even pay attention to the judgment of the rank and file, but when the chips are down (and in the Conservative party at all times and in the Labor party when it is in office the throwing of the chips is a prerogative of the leaders), all must toe the line. Thus in the Egyptian crisis of 1956, the country was bitterly divided, and not simply along party lines. There were plenty of Labor supporters who wanted to put Nasser in his place and plenty of Conservatives who doubted both the morality and the good sense of the government's policy. But how few members of parliament revealed anything of this deep division by their voices or their votes and how ill most of them failed when the party zealots punished them for acting as their consciences or their judgment dictated!

The member of parliament has many duties; some have been alluded to already. But he has one primary and overruling duty, to support or oppose the government of the day. It is a simple duty easily performed, but it does not call for much character or a high sense of citizenship and it is not unnatural that the critics see a falling off in the character of the House of Commons. Of course, there is and will be an adequate supply of adequate private members, backbenchers who do not wish or expect ministerial office, whose vanity or desire for public service at a pedestrian level or need for the not very lavish salary induces them to accept the burdens and endure the humiliations of the life of a modern member of parliament. It is probable that the level is a good deal higher than in local government, and it is certain that the local nominating committees take a more serious view of the qualifications of a prospective member of parliament than of the prospective alderman. But out of the House of Commons come the makers of present and future governments, and it may be that, in twenty years from now, we shall have to pay in a nearly universal mediocrity for the fact that for the young, ambitious, and independent man, a parliamentary career is no longer attractive and the voter duly exercising his right to vote, like a good citizen, has only to choose between King Log and King Stork.

What are the remedies? Some preach proportional representation, but the bias of the English people in favor of a simple electoral system is such that to ask for an electoral reform is to ask for the moon. And of course the present system suits the two great parties admirably. They cannot have their flank turned and, pivoting on the bases of their blocks of safe seats, they can fight their formal wars.

There is more to be said for and perhaps a slightly more hopeful cause to fight for in the adoption of some form of the primary system. For at present candidates are nominated by small party groups, necessarily unrepresentative, seeking as a rule the best man for the local party, not often enough the best man for the national party and never simply the best man.

But can we wonder that all parties and nearly all critics talk of apathy and lament the indifference of the elector who thinks he has done his duty when he has voted once every five years? As a citizen, this elector is certainly not overworked physically or mentally! He is not educated either.

Of course, the voter is to blame, not only for not demanding or supporting more independence, but for asking his representative to spend so much time on mere chores. It is not merely the prestige of local government that suffers for reasons already given. The prestige of parliament suffers, too. The member has the double duty of voting as his chiefs order and acting as a kind of consul or claims agent for his voters. It may be that it is not necessary to run errands for the voters. Some very experienced politicians like Lord Attlee think it is not. But if it is true that a member may get elected although he does not promise to run errands and may stay elected although he continues to refuse to run errands, it may be very hard to persuade a nominating committee to choose this modern version of Coriolanus or to renominate him if he does not play up to the new "service" conception of the duties of a member.

If the level of active cooperation in the running of local and national government has fallen, there has been a corresponding falling off in the role of the private societies whose importance was stressed earlier. There are many reasons for that. Some are simple and represent irreversible trends. Inflation, for example, has cut into the endowments of old "charities" (using the term in its wide legal sense). Thus some Oxford and Cambridge colleges have been on the edge of bankruptcy. The stipends of many Church of England vicars have shrunk in purchasing power until the parson is definitely declassed, worse off than many members of the "working class." Private hospitals, schools, orphanages, are in straits. And nothing can be done about this except to turn more and more of the responsibilities of the old private foundations over to the state. The Church of England amalgamates parishes until one parson has a large and unmanageable area to serve and is a barely recognizable figure in it. Local hospitals enter the state system; schools accept grants and a measure of control. This trend is a result of a great economic phenomenon that has gone still further in France and is visible in the United States. Inflation is one of the ineluctable facts of our time.

There is another phenomenon, harder to demonstrate but to me more significant. This is the decline in the functions of the churches as educators for citizenship. A generation ago, two generations ago, the "Nonconformist conscience" was a political force to reckon with. Today it puts on a brave front and, since politicians are notoriously timid, it wins a few victories or rather rearguard actions. But it is, for all that, a paper tiger. The churches are losing ground in membership, in prestige, in power. And yet they, especially the Nonconformist churches, were a great source of political education. It was not so much the nature of the causes they espoused but the fact that it was made the duty of a Christian man to have opinion on public issues and to do something about them. Needless to say, the real "activists" were always a minority, but they were a potent minority. Today they are still more of a minority and are nearly, if not quite, impotent.

I am less concerned with the decline in religious belief and fervor (that is an important but a different topic) than with the diminution of the political education given in the teaching and exemplification of the duties of citizenship in the political sense and with the diminution of the training given in the manning and working of the innumerable church-fostered organizations that gave so much of the color and flavor to English life. In serving these church bodies, the ordinary man or woman was taken out of his narrow round of house and job and given both a wider horizon and a wider range of duties and interests. It was because this was so that the English state could and did leave to private organizations so much that in France or Germany was automatically assumed to be the business of the state. But he gained more than that. He gained the idea that there were duties that he *ought* to fulfil which were not imposed by law or sanctioned by punishment. If, as the French believe, the English are superior to them in "civisme," here is one of the causes of the superiority. But to an alarming degree, the average man today sees it as a matter of "we" and "they," of orders coming down from above, more or less obeyed from below, not of orders given from within and obeyed for reasons that have nothing to do with the power of the state. It is not only the private organizations, most of them church-inspired, that suffer; it is also the body politic that is, in theory, based on the voluntary collaboration of good citizens to make the law and to obey it because they have made it.*

It would be absurd to pretend that all private action is rapidly declining. The trade unions have never been richer, had more members, exercised more power, been more treated as an estate of the realm. But the trade unions, too much at ease in Zion, find that it is hard indeed to get members to attend branch meetings, to develop policies from below, or to see in the unions not merely a means of getting better wages or working conditions but a new way of cooperative life. Strike discipline is excellent, even immorally excellent in some cases. Union leaders are, as a class, honest and competent to a degree that might breed envy in some American unions or, at any

---

* A possible casualty of this change is the idea of private charity. There are still numerous charities and there is much giving. (There would be more if the tax authorities permitted the English taxpayer to unload so much of his giving on the Bureau of Internal Revenue as the American system does.) But the state does more and more what the old charities did. There has consequently grown up the idea that the state does *all* that is required. The old Christian idea of the duty of charity is losing its hold. A friend of mine, a zealous Methodist and an important official, making inquiries in her office about having certain donations to charity deducted from her salary, discovered that *none* of her subordinates made any charitable contributions whatever.

rate, breed envy in those who have to deal with some American union leaders. But the pictures painted by the guild socialists just before the war of 1914 or by the syndicalists just after it seem remote and rosy today. The unions are a necessary part of the national way of doing business; they are not a new way of doing the nation's business. And when the unions have important business to do, they do it in a huddle in Whitehall, with the government or with the leaders of the corresponding bodies on the employers' side. For the union member, the union leaders are nearly as much "they" as the employers or the government. Again, a more rigorous system of ensuring the honesty of union elections, the imposition of quorums for important decisions, an increase in the number of active union members who are not Labor party members as well—all these things would restore life and some of the old crusading fervor to the unions. And it is still possible for the real union man who is willing to work as shop steward or union branch secretary to learn in union activities that there is more to citizenship than just voting. But how few are the men or women thus educated! Especially how few the women, for it would be unrealistic not to note that although women have long had the vote and in theory and largely in practice have had equal opportunity for jobs, the average woman still has her heart elsewhere, on getting and keeping a husband rather than on molding the policies of a union or of the nation. Indeed, since it is a universal complaint that young women will not devote to their duties as active members of unions or parties the time they devote to the proper study of man, it is sad that by limiting the duty of jury service to householders, the English system fails to draw on many middle-aged housewives of comparative leisure and with a sound knowledge of human nature.

But even if women were more commonly members of juries, that would only to a slight degree slow down the decline of the jury system. For it, "the palladium of English liberty," is in decline. It has nearly disappeared in civil cases, and where it still plays an important part, in libel actions for instance, the results are not always reassuring. It still has a great role to play in criminal actions, but even there, more and more cases are handled summarily without juries. From the jury came so much that has marked off the English political way of life from that of its neighbors! Parliament itself is a child of the jury, but the parent is a little like an old relative allowed to putter about the house but not to do serious business.*

If the failure of the trade unions to promote a new and ethically superior way of life is one disappointment in this era of prosperity and full employment, the cooperative movement has, for a decade past, stagnated. No more than the trade unions is it a way of life such as the pioneers dreamed of.

It is easy to blame the growth in mere size of the unions, of the cooperative wholesale societies—which is a necessary aspect of the modern economy, the

---

* One result of the decline of the jury system is to be noted, since it would scandalize a Frenchman. The Englishman "in trouble" or with a claim to put forward finds himself faced with either a solitary judge or a largely amateur bench of magistrates. The first would probably shock the Frenchman more than the second. The Englishman can, of course, appeal, but comparatively few do.

price we pay for its prodigal production. But when the prodigal production is itself of doubtful value or of undoubtful nonvalue, can we be consoled so easily? If the jury is declining, what of that other palladium, the press? Here it seems to many that it is not so much a matter of slow decline but of a Gadarene rush over the cliff edge. In the English liberal and still more in the radical theory of democracy and of the duties and possibilities of citizenship, as high a place was given to the role of the press as even Mr. Jefferson could have expected. The steady increase in "education," that is, in facilities for formal schooling, was expected to produce a more literate, competent, and public-spirited electorate. The facilities have not done so, or rather they have done so and have also done other things not so useful for the political health of the community. Many more people read, but what they read is not necessarily edifying. The sight of young soldiers reading (if that is the proper word) the "comics," largely American in origin, depresses the zealous democrat.*

Nor is he much more comforted by the sight of the actual reading that the popular press provides. The most popular newspaper in the world, with a circulation larger than *Pravda's, The News of the World*, concentrates on crime and sport; it caters visibly for very nonpolitical readers. And even those papers which combine a political "line" with immense

* It would not have surprised or, perhaps, depressed that sardonic conservative, the great Lord Salisbury, who said that the most visible result of universal education was that certain words were written lower down on the walls than they used to be.

circulation larger than *Pravda's, The News of the World,* for instance, do not expect much of their readers, whose power of concentrated attention is assumed to be that of a not very advanced schoolboy. Indeed, such phenomena have led exacerbated critics to assert that England has the worst popular press in the world. That is probably an exaggeration, but certainly a great part of the voting population gets little light or leading from the papers it reads. Nor are the other mass media notably better. In a moment of misguided enthusiasm after the late war, Miss Ellen Wilkinson, then a junior minister in the Ministry of Education, expressed the hope that England would become a "Third Programme country." But the famous highbrow program of the British Broadcasting Corporation has withered to a shadow, and now confronted with the television programs of the BBC and of the independent, "commercial" networks, the spectator has to remind himself that he is not in America, reduced to the lower offerings of American mass entertainment.

And it is assumed, without any very definite proof, that the increase in juvenile crime that is one of England's plagues, as it is one of America's, is in some way connected with the emptiness of the lives of the young that comics, television, even rock and roll, do not satisfactorily fill. Yet it must be remembered that the girls who shriek over famous Americans like Elvis Presley in a few years usually settle down and are absorbed in their children, husbands, and kitchens. (They may not be good citizens in the political sense, but they have ceased to be bad citizens in the police sense.) And we have acquired a better appreciation of the seamless web of family, of neighborhood. We no longer think that moving a mass of young people to new, elaborately fitted houses on the outskirts of the great cities will cure crime or fill empty lives. We may not know the solutions to the problems that face us but we are seeking less purely material solutions.

And, perhaps, we are concentrating less on the problem children, who are after all a minority. If universal literacy has produced the boys for whom the comics are all the "reading" they require, it has produced the probably more numerous groups who buy the paperbacks—including mearly a million copies of the *Odyssey*! If the present generation of young people is indifferent to politics, it is not totally a bad thing in a world that politics has nearly destroyed. The Hitler youth were not, alas, indifferent to politics nor are the drilled gun-toters of the so-called people's republics like East Germany.

Nor have we totally failed in meeting the new demands of the new society. By what is, I think, a brilliant piece of political invention, we have solved the problem of governmental aid to universities in terms that exclude political domination of the universities. The University Grants Committee, although appointed by the government, is not a government agency. It argues *for* the universities, tries to secure for them as much money as possible, but having got the money out of the Treasury, it has an absolutely free hand in spending it—and universities having got their grants are free, within very wide limits, to spend it as they choose. This autonomy is attacked by dogmatic purists among civil servants and by old-fashioned admirers of parliamentary control, but it seems to be in no danger; and under this extremely elastic system, the British universities have made immense progress. It is no part of the duties of a head of one of our universities to nobble or even to persuade legislators of the needs of the higher learning! At worst, he has to persuade an academic body in sympathy with his general, if not always with his particular, aims. The universities can choose how to serve the state, and this marriage of convenience is stable as far as one can foresee.

If there is too much power at the center, there is a healthy and, I believe, growing scepticism about the claims of the central authority to know best. If the private member of parliament is usually impotent, he can be formidable if he finds a genuine case of disregard of private rights by the police of a tiny Scottish burgh or a power-drunk government department. If there is too much concentration of policy-making at the center, the policy-makers have to deal with countervailing powers like the trade unions. And there are enough remaining organs of public opinion —great newspapers like the *Manchester Guardian*, the leaders of the churches, even voices raised in the torpid air of the House of Lords—to keep our rulers nervous if not frightened.

It seems to me that we must in England (and I think in other countries too) rethink our institutions. Given the necessarily national scale of business, we must have national government and national unions.

Given the close integration of the economy, we must accept the fact that in a country the size of Britain there can be only one effective tax structure, and that means central grants and a degree of central control.

We have other more difficult novelties to face. The old hierarchical order is dead in England (it died sooner, I think, in Scotland). We must accept the fact that most people will not devote much time or thought to politics, and that means that everywhere the active citizens will be a minority. We must make it more attractive for them to serve, and one way of making it more attractive is to give them real business to do. It is a healthy sign in England that the most lively local discussions are now over education, and it is in the field of education that local authorities show most signs of breaking the leading strings of the central government.

'Tis true, and pity 'tis, 'tis true, that many of the old organizing forces are weaker than they were, notably the churches, and I see no chance of their reviving. Yet we must watch out for any growing points in the new society that is coming up all around us. The world is always in an age of transition, but it is not merely banal to point out how rapid are the transitions of our age. We still live in old territorial forms, while it is likely that, in a few years, we shall see men landing on the moon. If we cling to old patterns, old institutions that are dead or dying, we shall see all power pass to "them" away from "us," even the power to complain effectively. It is a basic democratic belief that no one is fit to be trusted with uncontrolled power, that government by "meritocracy," to use the new English phrase, may be the most intolerable of all, driving men to regret the days of Bumble and the methods of Tammany Hall. We must build into our institutions points of resistance to the never-ending audacity of nonelected persons, in government bureaus, in union headquarters, and in the board rooms of business, big and not so big.

But the problem of citizenship is, in England as elsewhere, the problem of citizens. We must think hard and long about the ways in which we can, in our new world, preserve the virtues of the old. We shall not do so by clinging in desperate conservatism to the old ways. We shall have to find new ways to do old and good things. We must count the human cost of change, not refuse to pay it if we have to, yet not assume that we can get a brave new world on the cheap. Our danger at the moment in England is not blind optimism or black despair. It is an uneasy scepticism that passes the buck to the official, to the outsized organization. If I were asked in a single phrase to say what we need most in England today to revive the idea of citizenship, I should seriously say, "more cranks." I cannot believe that the race of cranks is dead, and as long as it is not, we shall have our urban Hampdens withstanding petty tyrants over many things, great and small. And we must fight over the small to save the great.

CITIZENSHIP IN FRANCE

PERHAPS THE EASIEST way to set out the problem of
citizenship in contemporary France is to point to the
revealing character of the national anthems in England, France, and the United States. The English
pray God to save the Queen, the embodiment in one
human being of the majesty and tradition of the state.
The Americans worship (I don't think the word is
extravagant) their flag, the emblem of union and of
national progress and power. And the French call on
the citizens of the republic to take arms in its defense.

"Aux armes, citoyens," is the appropriate theme
for a country so divided, that has suffered so much
from foreign and civil war, where the whole concept of
"citizenship" had to fight with the arms of the flesh
as well as of the spirit against the older concept of
"subject," where the general will of the people was set
up against the "good pleasure" of the king, where in a
cataclysmic outpouring of hope, energy, and courage
that, some hold with plausibility, exhausted the
nation for many generations:

> France in wrath her giant-limbs upreared
> And with that oath which smote air, earth,
>   and sea,
> Stamped her strong foot and said she would
>   be free.

She did more; she summoned the nations of the earth to imitate her and, with a boldness that the bolsheviks did not dare to emulate, announced a new era, "Year One of the Republic," and a new calendar in which the old pagan months and days, the Christian week itself, were discarded in favor of a new time for a new world.

And it is worth noting that if the revolutionary calendar is remembered at all today, it is for dates like Thermidor, Fructidor, Brumaire, that mark dates in a civil war which some hold is still going on in the heart of the French nation.

However that may be, the idea and the practice of citizenship cannot be the same as in a country like England where the national genius for the unclear combines the forms of feudal monarchy and the realities of advanced democracy, or the United States where the Revolution is sacred, is past, and is not to be recommenced. As Father Bruckberger once pointed out, the most astonishing thing about America for a Frenchman is the universal acceptance of the legitimacy of the American government. There is no nostalgia for the colonial past; there is not in the South any real belief that the "Lost Cause" can now be won. In the deepest sense of the word, the United States has a legitimate government. So has England, but no French government since 1789 has ruled with uncontested claims and few French governments could claim since that date to rule as the uncontested mandatories of the mass of the French people. In France no government is totally legitimate; no cause is fatally lost. Every Frenchman may accept his duty as a citizen, but in any group of three Frenchmen there will be two views of what those duties are. There may even be three, all incompatible, one with the other.

The basic point I am trying to make can best be illustrated by the contrast with England. In the Middle Ages, the two countries had the same legal language, French. They had closely similar institutions, as the common political vocabulary shows (parliament, court, jury). The Queen still gives her formal consent to laws in old French and the royal motto is still "Dieu et mon Droit." But these verbal resemblances are what dictionary makers call "false friends." The words look alike; they may even be identical; but they mean different things.

By 1789 the chance of salvaging "the ancient constitution" of France, of putting new life into the old medieval institutions that still existed, was dead. Even by the time that Montesquieu published the *Esprit des Lois* in 1748 it was probably too late. The French monarchy like Moses' rod had swallowed up the living corporate institutions in which France had been as rich as England. Old institutions survived, guilds, colleges, monasteries, local parliaments, local sovereign courts, but all real business was done "de par le roy," by royal authority. King Louis XVI, who patronized and probably saved the infant American republic, was not a Roman tyrant or a Russian autocrat, but he was the embodiment of a political system in which there were more duties than rights, and both were defined and allocated from above. There were subjects, not citizens, and from the be-

ginning of the Revolution, the concept of the "citizen" was an arm of political war, not the description
of an accepted status.

Just as it is impossible to understand the problem
of effective citizenship in contemporary England
without harking back to its historical roots, it is
impossible to understand the problem of citizenship
in contemporary France without harking back to the
kind of monarchy that was taken over by the
"People" between 1789 and 1792. The monarchy
had established all over France what was by the
standards of the age, or perhaps by any standards, an
efficient bureaucracy based on the principle that Paris
(or Versailles) knows best. Royal officials decided
what was good for the people they ruled, what came
to be called "les administrés." They built roads and
bridges, ran hospitals and jails. The old medieval
institutions survived in uneasy competition with or
in subordination to the royal officials. One great
independent corporation, the church, had its own
institutions, but they were usually subject to some
degree of royal control. There were cities and provinces with some degree of autonomy, but these relics
of a livelier past were not impressive for efficiency or
public spirit.

It was true that some of these corporate bodies
made desperate attempts to preserve or revive their
independent powers, but usually they did this in
defense of their local and particular interests. That
might make them momentarily popular as they re-
sisted the intrusions of royal power, but they had
little to offer the people who were outside the privi-

leged groups; and the men who had the clearest idea of what France needed were, in the main, hostile to these relics of a feudal past and in favor of a modern, "enlightened" central authority, at the moment necessarily a royal authority but capable of being exercised by officers not owing loyalty and obedience to the king. By 1789 the salvation of France was seen in the abolition of "privilege" and that meant the production of a uniform class of citizens, equally subject to the law and the active discouragement of any groupings of these citizens that would cut them off from their fellows and interrupt the direct impact of the will of the sovereign on every one of the twenty-five millions of Frenchmen. The tradition was established that in this way and in no other could a modern system of administration be created that would make available to the people the technical and moral advantages of the age.

Then the identification of the church with obscurantist policies and practices, its damnation by Voltaire as "l'infâme," the infamous thing, made it certain that the greatest of corporations would be brought to heel and that the very idea of independent church action parallel with and if necessary hostile to state action would be frowned on. The rendering of what was due to Caesar eclipsed what was due to God—if God was represented by the intolerant and often corrupt church. Then the persecution of the Huguenots that had so weakened France (if it had profited South Carolina and other bodies politic) had either exiled or driven into obscurity that section of the French bourgeoisie which was best fitted to make the transition into modern times. What was missing in eighteenth-century France was the chance of a Wesley to show himself and work his wonders, to give the education in citizenship that nascent Methodists gave to the masses of the English.

To avoid the reproaches of the pedantically accurate, I hasten to admit that the Revolution, in its beginning, gave very wide powers of autonomy to the new local government units it set up, and villages, towns, the new "départements" that replaced the old provinces, were, for a brief period, freed from effective central control. But not only was this period brief, the Revolution at the same time swept away all the intermediate bodies around which dangerous loyalties as well as often wasted wealth were assembled. The new man, the citizen, was sufficient unto himself. But that citizen was not in fact a uniform independent right-bearer. For the new regime as well as the old discriminated against the poor, against the worker as compared with the employer. Sweeping away feudalism meant sweeping away many rights and safeguards as well as abuses, and for many millions of Frenchmen, the confrontation of the simple citizen with the new omnicompetent state was far from being an education in independence and in civic virtue.

Then the local autonomy rashly granted in the first years of the Revolution was snatched away as war, foreign and civil, terror and counterterror, threats to national unity, religious persecution, invasion and revolt, forced on the revolutionary party the necessary instrument of dictatorship. Cities and departments, Lyon and Toulon, La Vendée and Morbihan, revolted, and it seemed that the choice was between tyranny and dismemberment and the triumph of the counterrevolution. When the dust settled under Bonaparte, the old royal institutions reappeared. Prefects took the place of intendants, Paris was more authoritative than it had ever been, and the power of the new state was greater and more untrammelled than the power of Louis XIV had ever been. The citizen was now ruled from above; he had little power of individual and no power of cooperative resistance to whatever regime had seized the levers of command of the central government.

In Paris, for example, was the headquarters of the uniform and highly centralized state education system. As the famous story put it, the minister of public instruction could take out his watch and say, "At this moment every boy of fourteen at school in France is doing geometry." The state educational system was designed to produce not merely scholars or technicians but good citizens; but the character, the claims, and the limits of good citizenship were decided from above.

In less important ways, the same command from the top was observable. France had the best roads and canals in Europe—but was much slower than her neighbors in getting railroads as the central authorities took a long time to decide what kind of railroads she should have. An efficient, uniform, monotonous, depressing uniformity marked French administration and local life, and initiative died under the shadow of Paris.

These weaknesses of the Napoleonic legacy were widely understood. The need for encouragement of local initiative, the need for giving a chance to private enterprise and expecting more from the good citizen than mere obedience, were some of the lessons Tocqueville brought back from America. The "tutelle administrative," the control by the agents of the central power of such local autonomy as was grudgingly permitted, prevented many mistakes and many of the abuses that moved Dickens to angry laughter in the England of his day; but if French government, locally administered under central control, was cheap, honest, and efficient in what it was permitted to do, it gave few opportunities to the energetic citizen to show by his own independent action that citizenship was more than obedience.

It would be an evasion (and an evasion making the understanding of contemporary France impossible) not to notice one reason why the central government frowned on individual, and still more on corporate, initiative. If men and women were allowed to supplement or to compete with the work of the state, the chief beneficiary would be the resurgent church. And the thought of a resurgent church frightened many who otherwise might have welcomed some counterpoise to excessive state power. Thus the chief rival to the cold and inadequate state system of charity was the reviving system of church charity, the orders of nuns and brothers, the great lay society of Saint Vincent de Paul. And these bodies, obedient to church authority, helped to strengthen the church that Bonaparte had hoped to turn into a

mere department of civil service by his Concordat.
He wanted a spiritual police; what he got was a
spiritual power. And that spiritual power, distrusted
on the eve of the Revolution, was still more distrusted
now. For between church and state lay the rivers of
blood shed in the Revolution. It matters nothing for
our purpose who was to blame. There was much on
each side to be forgiven, and the French, politically
speaking, do not forgive easily! Any recrudescence
of church power meant the possible danger of a revival of church claims, of a revival of intolerance, of
claims to pre-eminence, of control of the educational
system, for instance. Not only the atheists and
agnostics but most Protestants preferred leaving too
much power to the state (even in the private affairs of
the Protestant churches) than to risking any revival
of Catholic authority.

In England, the great efflorescence of religious
activity that we can conveniently in a kind of historical shorthand associate with the coming of
Methodism and the Evangelical revival in the Church
of England meant that the churches were the auxiliaries of the state, did much that the state might have
done, trained their adherents in all kinds of public
works, and bred in them unconscious public spirit.
In France, the church watched and, harassed by the
state as far as it succeeded in creating its own system
of schools, charities, organizations of piety and
mutual help, did so, at the best, in face of grudging
tolerance and at the common worst of persecution
irritating enough to breed the spirit of martyrdom

and not effective enough to destroy the roots of the danger (if there was a danger) to the lay state.

Thus in a very large body of Frenchmen, more ready than not to spend their own time and their own money on public or quasi-public objects, there was bred the spirit of hostility to and suspicion of the state. As little as possible should be given to the public authorities that the more might be given to God or the church. The very classes and the very human types that in England, unconsciously as well as consciously, made the transition to democracy easy were in France barely tolerant of the state (and barely tolerated by it) and were profoundly suspicious of a democracy to which were attributed the sins of the Terror and the threat of a renewal of the horrors of 1793. When we remember how often pious French men and women were sent into exile or when we remember that in 1848 and in 1871 the archbishop of Paris was among the chief victims of civil war, we can understand Catholic fears and resentments; but the fact remains that the loyalties of many of the most public-spirited Frenchmen were divided—to the loss of the concept and practice of good citizenship in France.

Nor was the threat from or to the church the only cause of division, the only reason why the exorbitant power of the French State was tolerated or approved of by many honest and intelligent citizens. France was a country both threatened by external and menaced by internal war. The form of government changed every twenty years or so, and every change opened the gates to violence and civil war. In the great cities, notably in Paris, there was the continual danger of a "red" revolution made by the desperate poor of the slums—and not only by them but by quite respectable citizens who had seen, so they thought, the hopes of the Revolution frustrated. After the June Days of 1848, after the Commune of 1871, could any serious citizen propose to give real autonomy to Paris? Might not the overmighty city proceed from autonomy to independence, even to the conquest, in the name of the Revolution, of the passive countryside? So intelligent conservatives argued (and even to this day no French government has dared give complete autonomy to Paris, complete control of the police, for example).

Then after the great disaster of 1870, after the catastrophe of invasion and dismemberment followed by civil war, it was highly doubtful whether France, weakened and in constant danger, could give to local authorities an autonomy that might interfere with the national defense. Even after mayors were elected, not nominated, a main part of their duties was to organize recruitment for the army and carry out the orders of the central government given through the prefects. And mayors with these duties had to be more strictly controlled than mayors in less threatened societies like England or the United States. So we find parties in opposition preaching decentralization and, once in power, keeping the control of local government in their own safe hands. And meantime, as in the past, local initiative was stifled and the good citizen stayed at home and minded his own business.

Yet things moved. The new trade unions, grudgingly tolerated, began to create loyalties and exercise
power outside the framework of the state. The
worker's political education thus promoted may not
have been wide, but the loyalties evoked were deep.

But the formal organization of the governmental
system concealed some profound changes. The powers
of cities and departments might be rigorously limited;
their legal activities might be controlled, even in
petty detail, by prefects and subprefects, but with
the establishment of parliamentary government after
1870, it became more and more important to notice
who manned the local government bodies. It became the rule, in practice, for every aspiring deputy
to be a member of his local council. If he was an
important deputy, he was usually a mayor or the
chairman of the departmental council. As such he
could by his power and prestige in Paris limit the
power of the prefects. A prefect of the Rhone who
failed to notice that the mayor of Lyon was M.
Édouard Herriot, repeatedly president of the Cham-
ber of Deputies, would not remain prefect of the
Rhone for long. A politician learned how much
stronger was his position in Paris if he had a strong
position in local government at home. And that, in
turn, led to an ambitious politician securing more
power for the body or bodies which were politically so
important to him. Even before the war of 1914,
French local government was more lively, breeding
more interest, giving opportunity for more initiative,
than the text-books would suggest. The ways in
which a powerful politician built up his base had

many American parallels, and to describe the French governmental system without noticing this interplay of national and local politics would be like describing the formal government of New York without mentioning Tammany Hall.

There was one important difference to be noted, however, between New York and Lyon or the Meuse. French local government was both honest and thrifty. Too thrifty, it might be said, for many social services taken for granted in Germany or England were not provided for at all or were starved in France. Yet the move toward local autonomy went on.

For example, the rigorously centralized "university" slackened some of its bonds. The rigorously controlled and rigorously separated "Faculties" in the provinces were reunited into universities with some degree of autonomy and, for example, with the power of receiving and administering gifts. The "climate of opinion" moved in the direction of autonomy. Legal theorists invented doctrines that supported the autonomy of trade unions and all other types of societies. Or all other types but one, for the church was still suspect and the years just before the first world war saw the greatest rigors exercised against the church or rather against the auxiliary institutions into which so much of French wealth and public spirit was poured.

Yet a Frenchman who might be called on to serve on a jury, who might run for office and find a field for dignified service in local government, who could now collaborate with other Frenchmen in the promotion of common objects, was far from the passive "administré" of the time of Tocqueville. He had recognized duties to more than the central government, and that government, more or less grudgingly, accepted the steady diminution of its once unquestioned authority.

The first world war was for France the great catastrophe of this century, the great catastrophe after the Revolution. By desperate, heroic, and almost fatally exhausting efforts, France was saved, but at a terrible price. Yet it was not all loss. The necessities of war imposed all kinds of improvisation, and if more was still left to the state than in England or America, the habit of private organization and cooperative effort grew. Moreover, the old quarrel between church and state seemed absurd and meaningless, indeed odious, in face of the terrible calamity that had befallen the country and in face of the heroic contribution of priests, nuns, and brothers to the common cause. The religious orders were allowed to come back; an agreement was come to with the Vatican. The Catholics, so long alienated or self-exiled from many forms of public life, came back; this was especially important in local government, where the priest, the bishop, was no longer automatically the enemy of the prefect or the mayor. Church and state were now ready at times to collaborate; the church made fewer claims and the state showed less jealousy of the action of the church.

But if this was a gain for the wider concept of citizenship, there was a great loss to be offset against the gain. For from this time dates the final alienation of the French workers because of the rise of the Communist party. It is perhaps wrong to attribute the alienation to the rise of the Communist party. The rise was due to the pre-existent alienation. Since the Commune of 1871, so savagely suppressed, the militant French workers had seen in the bourgeois state an enemy, not an ally. The golden expectations of the great Revolution had been repeatedly deceived and the workers, excited by the promises made during the great war, were eager for their fulfilment. But the triumphant French State, desperately poor and unconscious of the needs of what was still a novel minority, the working population of the great industrial towns, postponed all serious consideration of the new claims, fell back on an old-fashioned nationalism, and made it certain that the brilliant if deceptive promises of the bolshevik Revolution would be taken at their face value by the militant workers. That the bolshevik promises were "pie in the sky" was soon evident, but the French worker had lived on a diet of such pie for over a century. He was not alienated by its nonnutritious character now.

Be that as it may, the political leadership of a great part of industrial and of some part of rural France passed into the hands of the Communists, who were able to use the new freedom of local government to dig themselves in and to finance the party. French local government had been honest but excessively thrifty. This had meant that in many of the fast growing towns, social services were grossly inadequate. The Communists' taking over did, in fact, provide for many real wants and earned real gratitude. For hard as it may be to believe in the United

States, many of the recruits to the French Communist
party were honest, public-spirited, optimistic if naïve
men and women. And they found in the service of
the party in local government the means of expression
of a genuine public spirit and the means of meeting
real social needs.

But the price was high. For the Communist
leaders, as the events of 1939 were to show, were
docile tools of the policy of the Soviet government
and it was their interest to alienate the French workers from the mass of the French nation. To a con-
siderable degree they succeeded in their aim. The
Communist-controlled cities became enclaves inside
the nation, run by the party for the party. The
general funds of the municipalities helped, by various
ingenious tricks, to pay much of the cost of party
propaganda, and whenever it suited party policy the
powers and resources of the local authorities were
used to aid the party and to thwart and undermine
the authority and policy of the central government.
This was made easier by the identification of the
rival organizers of society, the churches, with the
employers. The Catholic Church had long been,
although in recent years with less justice, associated
with business. And if Protestant employers had been
able to ally themselves with radical movements up to
the war of 1914, the case was altered when being on
"the left" meant submission to bolshevik leadership.

The Communists were able to withdraw a great
part of the nation from the nation. And whereas it
had been roughly true to say that before the war of
1914 only the Catholic Church had been able to

organize private associations for charity, education, or sport, on any great scale, the Communists showed that they could compete too. They had their equivalents of Sunday schools, their boy scouts, cycling clubs, football teams, their night schools and summer schools for indoctrination. As far as they could— which was pretty far—they aimed at creating a Communist climate in which children should grow up to whom loyalty to the party meant more than loyalty to the French republic or to France.

For the old unquestioning patriotism that had united Catholic and Protestant, royalist and republican, had suffered terribly in the first world war. The great reaction against war that followed the war of 1914-18 was deeper in France than in most other countries, naturally, since France had suffered far more than most other countries. As the fruits of victory proved sour and indigestible, there was a growing scepticism about the old dogmas. Men doubted if the whole sum of civic duty was summed up in the patriotic poem that asserted that a Frenchman should live and die for France. Live, yes, but die?

The Communists, by no means pacifist themselves, exploited this sentiment. And since in France, after the great Revolution, patriotism of a naïvely militant sort had been the republican religion, its decline weakened the moral power of the State. Men cherished loyalties other than that owed to the state, and the State of the Third Republic was not dignified enough to win much automatic loyalty or respect.

Then came the second world war. It was a moral catastrophe as the first war had been a material catastrophe (although the material losses and the losses of life were great in the second war, they were not as overwhelming as the losses of the first war). There was, first of all, the catastrophe of sudden, unexpected, complete, and humiliating defeat, a defeat attributed too dramatically to French disunion instead of to German superiority in weapons and military skill. The spectacle of the leaders of a great party, the Communists, suddenly changing sides and preaching peace (which meant surrender) when they had been preaching war and not being disowned, effectually, by the the rank and file was a revelation of the weaknesses of French citizenship.

But more damage was done by the establishment of the Vichy regime. It is probably true that this regime was welcomed by most Frenchmen in 1940. But it carried the seeds of its own dissolution in it. Its so-called National Revolution was never a serious affair, not even a serious Fascist affair, but it was authoritarian. The preaching of unlimited confidence in Marshal Pétain was the negation of the slow growth of the idea of the citizen managing his own local affairs and having a voice in the management of national affairs. The citizen was again a subject.

But worse was to come. The stupor of 1940 wore off; the Resistance began to grow, and allegiance was divided between it and the more and more discredited government of Vichy. There was no doubt (despite the thesis of some ingenious and patriotic lawyers) that Vichy was the legitimate heir of the Third Republic. Was it not recognized as such by the United States? There was no doubt, either, that it was a German convenience and more and more a German tool. To sabotage the work of the Vichy government became, for a greater and greater number of energetic Frenchmen and Frenchwomen who had found their leader in General de Gaulle, the first duty. That might mean taking to the Maquis and fighting not merely Germans but the Vichy militia. France, again, knew the horrors and the moral dangers of civil war. It might mean serving two masters, ostensibly working for the Vichy government but in reality serving the allied cause and the growing Resistance movement. In that case it meant a breach of formal discipline and duty; it meant mendacity, breach of faith. Men learned to undo at night the work they did during the day, to prepare the downfall of a government that they had sworn to serve. It meant the use of false papers, the utilization and the organization of the black market, the "removal" of traitors by methods close to murder. It meant the division of family against family, of brother against brother. It meant what can only be called a patriotic demoralization, necessary, courageous, noble, but deplorable.

And the French case differed from that of the other occupied countries. They had their "governments in exile." The Quislings had no moral status or plausible appeal. But the head of the legal French government was a great French hero and he was in France, while his rival was a hardly known soldier, condemned to death, living in London and then in Algiers. No wonder the French people were bewildered. Thousands of lives were lost at the hands of the Germans and of the Vichy militia who behaved worse than all but the worst of the Germans. So when liberation came, there was a country riddled with conspiracy, where few knew what was the real seat of power, where there were terrible scores to be paid off, and where there was immense material damage to be undone as well as moral reconstruction to be undertaken.

Liberation meant revenge. Thousands more perished, many no doubt unjustly; thousands more were disgraced, and some of them had done no more than serve the legal government. And the necessary bad civic habits of the underground survived to plague the liberated country.

There was one other handicap under which the French state suffered and which made the French attitude to citizenship ambiguous. After the German invasion of Russia, the Communists in France turned about and, entering the Resistance, became some of the bravest, most successful, most admired actors in the drama. "Entering the Resistance" is not quite the right phrase, for the Communists carefully kept their own underground organization intact and separate while they tried to infiltrate the other underground organizations. It is possible, although I think it unlikely, that the Communists might have taken over France as they later took over Czechoslovakia. But there were two obstacles in the way. There was the military authority of General Eisenhower and the political authority of General de Gaulle. General Eisenhower could not permit the usurpation of authority in his lines of communication, and General de Gaulle, with great boldness and political sense, took over the command of the Resistance, replaced the vanished government of Marshal Pétain, and, dissolving the Communist and other private armies, restored the authority of the French state or, as he would have put it, of the republic whose abolition by Pétain he had always refused to recognize.

General de Gaulle was forced to accept Communists in his government, but he carefully excluded them from the basic ministries—Defense, Foreign Affairs, and, above all, the Interior, which controlled the police. France was saved from a Communist dictatorship and the provisional government was soon to have its authority ratified by popular vote. But it had been, as the Duke of Wellington said of Waterloo, "a close run thing." And the basic problem remained. The authority of the republic had to be restored and the torturing ambiguities of the situation, as it affected the average Frenchman, had to be resolved. He had to be given an authority to obey; he had to be given duties as well as rights to observe and exercise. A concrete meaning had to be given to the word "citizen." And the miracle has been that so much success has been achieved in a task that in the divided, apparently ruined, drifting country of 1944-45 might well have seemed impossible.

It would not have been absurd to despair of the reconstruction of the authority of the French state and the effective restoration of the idea of the combination of rights and duties that we call citizenship —and there were observers, inside and outside France, who did despair. But the despair was premature, and I think it can be said that the standard of citizenship and the richness of the content of the concept in contemporary France show an improvement, not a decline.

How did this come about? Partly it is an example of the truth of Adam Smith's little joke. There *is* "a lot of ruin in a nation." But there are other forces at work than the famous French power of recuperation.

First and foremost, I should put the bringing of Frenchwomen into political life. For it was an inevitable result of the occupation and the Resistance that Frenchwomen should, at last, get the vote both in national and local elections. They had provided some of the most heroic leaders of the Resistance and some of the most glorious martyrs. Millions of women had kept the farms, shops, factories, going despite the absence in captivity of more than two million men. France had been largely saved from irreparable collapse by her women, and in the flux of the period of liberation, it was decided, almost without opposition, to admit women to full political rights.

It is my conviction that this decision more than offset the damage done by the occupation and by the necessarily devious methods of the Resistance. For Frenchwomen, when they had the vote, developed or revealed an interest in tangible reforms that offset the too theoretical passions of their menfolk. Women, even Communist women, were not ready to postpone all immediate ameliorations to the final solution of revolution. They turned out to want much the same things as American or English women. They wanted better schools, better medical treatment for children, better provision for poor and large families, better housing, and what may be loosely called general moral legislation. Thus it was, I am convinced, the woman voter who secured the abolition of legalized brothels, the ending of tolerated red-light districts, and the lavish system of family allowances which has been, if not the cause of the sudden and unforeseen rise in the French birth rate (the most important thing that has happened in France since the war), at any rate a guarantee that the bigger families would not push poor parents over the edge into real misery and has even made the lot of the young mother of middle-class origins easier than it would have been. It is, I believe, to the political weight of the woman's vote that French politics, local and national, have owed their increased practicality. And because of that increased practicality, the concept of citizenship has had more real meaning than it had when it found expression in vague, rhetorical terms. If before the war a municipality showed willingness to spend money on, for example, a new water supply or public housing, one was inclined to assume that it was dominated by the Communists. No such easy assumption is possible now. It is dominated in all probability by the need to please the women who are active in local politics both as voters and as councillors, mayors, and municipal leaders in general.*

* I went some years ago to a great cattle fair in central France in the company of a friend of mine, the owner of what is by French standards a big and very modern farm. I noted not only that the peasants who were selling their cattle were buying a lot of modern machinery (an unheard of thing before the war) but that their wives were buying washing machines. Since I knew that many of the villages had no water supply, that washing was done in a brook or a

The next great force making for a richer concept and practice of citizenship has been the Catholic Church. No longer is it automatically ranked as a conservative, reactionary force. The young priests are for the most part devotees of the "social gospel" and see their duties, in town and country, in social as well as in purely religious terms. It is in the most Catholic parts of France that the equivalents of American Four-H clubs flourish most, that rural education, after school age, in good farming practice shows most promise. It is also said, with what truth I know not, that the ministers of the Calvinist church, the "Reformed Church," receive too purely intellectual a training and in those areas where rural Protestantism is strong, mainly in the South, the minister, unlike the priest, is not as a rule a social leader, a curious reversal of the traditional picture. Be that as it may, the reconciliation between church and state has meant that there is far more effective collaboration than there was and that the public-spirited Frenchman is not as conscious as he was of divided and frustrating loyalties.

Yet of course one great ground of division remains, the Communist bloc, the political power of what General de Gaulle calls "the dissidents," the members and camp followers of a party that hardly pretends to put France first.

For some years after the liberation the Com-

---

pond, I asked my friend why they were so foolish. He replied that they were not necessarily foolish, that they were all voters, and that if enough women in a village invested in washing machines, they would see to it that the local man-dominated council put in a piped water supply.

munists were able to exploit their record in the Resistance. For example, some of the Catholic leaders of the Resistance were very reluctant to break with the Communists, not only because of old associations, but because of the danger of cutting the church off from the workers. Intellectuals of the left like Sartre continually suppressed their criticisms of Communist policy since that again might have meant alienation from the workers. Left to themselves, the French Communist leaders might have continued to play this double game with success, to pose as a French party of fundamental reform. But the increasing rigors of Stalinist foreign and domestic policy revealed too clearly the subservience of the French party to Russian leadership. It became harder and harder to ignore the servility of the French Communist leaders, harder and harder to find grounds for collaboration with them.

With the expulsion of the Communist ministers from the government in 1947, the issue was made clear. During their period of collaboration in the government, the Communists had managed to "colonize" certain important government departments, filling them with their own nominees whose basic loyalty was to the party, not to the government that employed them. A process of "decolonization" now began, and after a few years the governmental services were purged of these ambiguous servants. At the same time the violence of the Communist reaction to the setting up of NATO, as earlier to the establishment of the Marshall Plan, made it plain to all but the most willingly blind that the Communist party was not a normal French party but an instrument of Soviet policy. As far as this was made clear, the duty of a good French citizen was made clear, and that duty forbade collaboration with the Communists.

But the facts remained that millions of Frenchmen and Frenchwomen voted the Communist ticket, that hundreds of thousands remained faithful party members, subject to party discipline, and that all over France there was a network of open dissent and covert conspiracy. To bring back into the body of the French nation these lost sheep was obviously one of the main tasks of any responsible French government. But the weakness and instability of the short-lived ministries which marked the history of the Fourth Republic did not make this task an easy one. The weakness of the French state kept many people in the Communist ranks, since the Communists at least promised and could deliver authority and offered a coherent plan of political action.

At the same time, General de Gaulle's "Rally of the French People" attracted millions who were distressed by the weakness of the State and anxious for coherent leadership. Faced with these two dangers, communism and Gaullism, the parliamentary politicians passed electoral laws which were designed to give artificial strength to the central parties and in effect to disfranchise a great part of the Communist and Gaullist electors. This ingenious device succeeded for the time being in "saving the republic," but it greatly lessened the moral credit of the successive governments in the eyes of the average

Frenchman. He felt little loyalty or respect for the actual incumbents of transitory power in Paris, and the good citizen was often highly sceptical of the claims of his temporary rulers to respect or obedience.

The contrast between the very rapid economic revival of France and the feebleness of the government made for confusion in French public opinion. The Monnet plan and the Schuman plan for a European coal and steel pool were signs of energy and grounds for hope; but the political system got very little credit for the recovery of France. The engineers and other technicians who were giving France brand-new industrial equipment felt no gratitude to the French State, which, if it provided the means for the great reconstruction, seemed to have little idea of whither France was to go. Moreover, the old rural, small-town, and stagnant economy of France in which most French political habits had been formed, was giving way to a modern and technically very advanced urban society. For the young people leaving school and college, conscious of the immense opportunities that the new technology presented, old-fashioned party loyalties and old-fashioned ideological passions seemed uninteresting. Even the quarrels and heroism of the Resistance were passing into the background. The politicians complained that young people lacked party fervor. The Communists, as much as other parties, found it hard to win or keep the young, and there were complaints on all hands of the Americanization of French life. And one aspect of that Americanization was the substitution of concrete and immediate economic objects for the vague ideological programs which had been the delight and the deception of Frenchmen in the past. It is an apparent paradox but a real truth to say that the refusal of young Frenchmen and young French-women to take party programs too seriously was a sign of health and a proof of political wisdom. Men and women engaged in the material reconstruction of France were conscious of being as good citizens as if they had spent their time in political propaganda. And if they spent a great deal of their leisure in the enjoyment of such cultural importations as rock and roll, they might have spent their time worse, in partisan politics which kept alive national divisions.

Indeed, the old idea that the sole duty of a French citizen was to France was more and more questioned. The disasters of 1940 had shown that France could not stand alone. The disasters had also shown that the old France, dear to Conservatives and to tourists, of vineyards and picturesque villages, could not survive as a truly independent society in the modern world. The necessity of international organizations like NATO, the success of Marshall aid, proved for all open-minded Frenchmen that the future of France must lie in some degree of close cooperation with her neighbors.

Amid the ruins of 1945, the idea of "Europe" took root. The idea of a federation linking together former friends and enemies, ending centuries-old quarrels and creating a political organization powerful enough to look the two giants, the United States and the Soviet Union, in the face, took root especially among the young. The old patriotism was not enough, not even the patriotism of the Resistance. A new European patriotism was called for and under the threat of the atomic bomb perhaps even a world patriotism. There was a cleavage between the adherents to the old way of life, to the old stagnant French economy, and to the old narrow French patriotism and those, mainly to be found among the young, who knew that France must modernize or sink into an ineffectual stagnation and that true modernization is possible only in an ambit wider than that of the French nation.

As has been said, a simple and exclusively French patriotism had been the religion of good republicans. True, in the revolutionary tradition there was an element of universality. The sacred principles of 1789 applied in theory to the whole human race, but in practice they were applied pretty exclusively to Frenchmen. It was easy to talk of the French nation as consisting of a hundred million Frenchmen, that is, computing the subjects in the colonies in the arithmetic of the French state; but the inhabitants of the colonies were nearly all subjects, not citizens, and little effort was made to integrate them into the French nation. By 1945, if there ever had been a chance for such integration, it had been lost. Nationalism was on the move all over the French empire. General de Gaulle during the war had made promises of equality and liberty which had not been forgotten. In the Far East, in Indo-China, it was obvious that the people of what was now called Vietnam had no intention of accepting even the rank of French citizens as their political terminus. And this was

proved in a long, expensive, and disastrous war which
was bitterly and painfully educational. If the old
idea of a French citizen having no duties save to the
French state was becoming archaic, the newer idea of
all the former subjects of France being content to
become French citizens in some kind of federation in
which the final power should still rest with France
was visibly outdated.

The lesson of Indo-China was reinforced by the
outbreak of rebellion in Algeria. Here the contrast
between fiction and fact was most flagrant. Technically, Algeria was part of France, organized in three
departments which were supposed to be like the
Nord or the Puy-de-Dôme. Technically, since 1945,
all the inhabitants of Algeria were French citizens and
had the vote. For long the Algerian departments had
been represented in the Paris parliament, and now
there were representatives of all classes of the Algerian population sitting in the Palais Bourbon.

But the facts were very far from the theory. The
departments across the Mediterranean were not only
geographically remote from France, they were also
cut off from it by language, religion, and culture.
The Algerians who were really French citizens were a
small "white" minority, long accustomed to regarding
themselves as the masters and the spokesmen of
Algeria and very reluctant to admit to even formal
equality the great mass of Arabic-speaking Moslems.
As for their admission to real equality, the mere idea
was intolerable.

The Algerian war, and the problems it revealed
and created further tested the French idea of citizen-

ship. It was notorious that in Algeria the elections in the "Moslem colleges" were rigged by the administration. It was notorious that there was in effect a color bar operating to the disadvantage of the majority. Even on paper, the white minority had the same political weight as the great Arab majority. In practice, it had more, and in addition to its political superiority it had virtually complete command of all the economic resources of the country.

This was no novelty. What was a novelty was the rise of Arab nationalism and the great crisis of conscience which the Algerian war caused and causes in France. In 1945, the leaders of the Algerian Moslems would have been content with true equality and with full admission to the rank of French citizens. It was only when this was denied them that they turned to the creation of an Algerian nationalism based on Arabic and based, less openly, on the Moslem religion which, like the language, united them to their neighbors to the west and to the east, Morocco and Tunisia. When the government of the Fourth Republic, after a series of outrageous blunders, accepted independence for Morocco and Tunisia, it was too late to pretend with plausibility that Algeria was or could become simply part of France.

But equally important and perhaps more interesting for the light it casts on the changing attitude of Frenchmen in France to the concept and duties of citizenship was the increasing moral disquiet caused by the methods of repression used in the Algerian war. A French equivalent of the English "Nonconformist conscience" appeared, embodied in the

French church. One of the most effective critics of the methods of repression was the archbishop of Algiers, and he was supported by many of his colleagues in France. French Catholic papers like the daily *La Croix* not only reported candidly and severely on the conduct of the war but mobilized consciences against the belief that in this type of war any methods were tolerable. The group of young zealots who had as their organ *Témoignage Chrétien* gave their "Christian witness" by campaigning, in season and out of season, for a truly fraternal attitude to the Algerians in Algeria and in France. The old clash between the things that were due to Caesar and the things that were due to God was made more acute. Indeed, it could be said that the church did more to defend Christian and republican values than most of the lay parties did. Patriotism, especially patriotism based on barely concealed doctrines of race superiority, was now declared not to be enough. It would be absurd to pretend that this new doctrine was universally well received. Many Catholics resented the help given to Algerians, in Algeria and France, by priests and nuns. Others resented the fact that some of the most telling criticisms of the conduct of the French army came from army chaplains. But few could have predicted in 1914 that the Catholic Church would be a most effective critic of French policy in the French Empire. And there can be little doubt that the sense of shame which began to grow in France, as more was known of the nature of repression in Algeria, owed a great deal to the courageous witness of the church and to the acceptance of the idea that a Christian citizen has more duties than and different duties from those that the state defines and demands.

If the Algerian war ate away certain traditional illusions about the success of French policies in North Africa, the movement of history presented fresh problems in the colonies south of the Sahara. True, the situation was not as complicated and solutions were not as hard to find as in Algeria. Many of the Africans in the tropical colonies were Christians; especially was this true of the educated élite which the French had deliberately created. There was no unified Arab culture as in North Africa and no independent states like Morocco and Tunisia. There was little anti-French feeling, and for the educated élite, France was the source of modern culture. Some literary men preached a doctrine of "négritude," an exaltation and reconstruction of the African past, but they preached it in French. The great new ports were French creations, and into West Africa the French after the war poured a great part of their not very abundant capital surplus. There was far more possibility of a *modus vivendi* between France and these colonies than there was in North Africa.

The institutions set up after 1945 to give some kind of unity to the "French Union" had proved sickly creations. But many African leaders got the habit of visiting Paris on the business of the Union, of attending the impotent Union parliament, and they were divided between the attractions of total independence and the glamor of membership in what was to be called the "French Community." The common language of the colonies was French, and it was more difficult to conceive of new nationalities in tropical Africa than in the Maghrib, the three countries of North Africa. But again, if the leaders of the tropical colonies were proud to be French citizens, they were not content to be merely French citizens. They were not content to leave all final decisions to the "metropolis." They had the example of the British colonies now attaining or well on the way to independence. They could not settle for less than an equivalent status with that of Ghana, and so the French public learned, with some bewilderment and some distress, that being a French citizen in Dakar was a very different thing from being a French citizen in Bordeaux.

The evolution not only of tropical Africa but of other colonies like the great island of Madagascar toward an independent status might have been delayed but for the upheaval in Algiers which ended the life of the Fourth Republic. The Algerian war poisoned the life of the republic, morally as well as economically. The overthrow of governments in Paris for often trivial reasons, which caused no more than a shrug in France, increased the contempt of the white population of Algeria for the politicians of the metropolis. These "colons" were more than ever determined to be masters in what they thought was their own house. And so France was treated to the spectacle of an open revolt against the legal government starting in Algiers on May 13, 1958, and revealing the very limited degree of control which the civilian government in Paris had over the army in Algeria. Out of that crisis came the return to power of General de Gaulle and the creation of the Fifth Republic. The details of the Gaullist revolution and of the Gaullist constitution do not concern us, but it should first of all be noted that the government of General de Gaulle, both in the referendum on the constitution and in the election of the assembly that followed, got an overwhelming mandate with no parallel in modern French history. For once, France had a government whose moral and political authority was unquestioned. General de Gaulle carried every commune in France except one, including all the Communist strongholds. The nation was tired of disunion and of the political game that seemed more and more a concern of professionals and less and less the affair of the citizens.

Although the aim of the Gaullist revolution or, if that word is too dramatic, the Gaullist reform was to strengthen the authority of the State, the text of the constitution showed how much care had been devoted to the preservation of the fundamental rights of the citizen and how much power, in a negative sense at any rate, had been given to the parliament. The new constitution of 1958 was very far from being a dictatorial constitution, and indeed it could be said that there was some danger that after the death or retirement of General de Gaulle the Fifth Republic might slip only too easily into the old bad habits of the Fourth. The text of the constitution did not guarantee France against such a relapse and it did not give France the presidential government on the

American plan which many people had wanted and which many people thought was General de Gaulle's own ideal of government.

Taking advantage of the full powers granted by the dying assembly of the Fourth Republic, the government of General de Gaulle put into effect a great many reforms—most of them unimportant by themselves but becoming important by their number and mass—which had lain in the offices of government departments for years simply because no government had the courage to put them through. These decrees were usually the work of what, in an American sense, can be called "technocrats," the extremely able civil servants who had been frustrated in their reforming activity by the impotence of the old governmental system. And there were some who feared that France would be governed by technocrats, no doubt efficiently and no doubt to immediate economic advantage, but with the concurrent danger of a drying up of democratic spirit.

It was soon seen that these fears were superfluous. There was good reason to believe that General de Gaulle himself regretted the overwhelming tidal wave that filled the new assembly with "Gaullists." He had forbidden any party to use his name in the elections and had tried to secure the return to the assembly even of such obstinate critics of the new regime as M. Mendès-France. (Indeed, this was one of the few cases in history in which an administration has tried to gerrymander election districts in order to secure the election of opponents!) But the electorate was more Gaullist than the general; it unseated many or most of the old parliamentary leaders and sent into the new assembly hundreds of newcomers to French political life.

There was much alarm expressed and there were some grounds for the alarm that France was going into a dictatorial epoch. But these fears were soon seen to be groundless. For the French electors who had insisted in returning this Gaullist majority to back up the general in whatever he should decide to be for the interest of France acted quite differently when the elections to local government bodies took place. When it came to choosing a mayor or a councillor, the French elector firmly refused to believe that being a Gaullist was all that mattered. The attempt of M. Jaques Soustelle to repeat, on the municipal scale, his successes of the parliamentary elections failed. All over France, the electors chose local men and women whom they knew, whose services they had come to trust to manage local affairs. It is one of the paradoxes in the French idea of citizenship that the instability of the central government under the old regime was offset by the astonishing stability of local government. Once a French village or small town, or even a big town, had found a mayor who was trusted, it remained loyal to him through all the vicissitudes of national politics. The case of the father of Marshal de Lattre de Tassigny who was mayor of his village for more than sixty years is exceptional; but the tenure of local office as twenty or thirty years was not at all exceptional.

The local elections of 1959 showed that the voters were still loyal to their old local leaders (who in many cases had been national leaders as well). The roots of local government and local freedom and the attitude that made local issues paramount in local elections proved to be deeper than the fearful had asserted. The French voter, male and female, showed the political intelligence and the civic virtue required to save local government from being absorbed by the new and very powerful state that had been created in Paris. This meant of course that the Communists, so badly defeated in the parliamentary elections, kept their hold of a good many towns and cities. This was a high price to pay for proving the vitality of local government, but it was not too high a price. And since the new Senate was elected by the delegates of local government bodies, many old leaders returned to national political life.

To sum up, the French people managed to support the creation of an effective central government without either abandoning the essential liberties of the republican system or giving up their control of their own local business, which they continued to wish to be managed by local men whom they knew and trusted, not by either the new Gaullist politicians or the technocrats.

But what of the central government thus set up? It has the immense advantage of a genuine popular mandate and consequently has been able to do, not merely promise to do, many things that all Frenchmen know need to be done. It has been able to stand up to various pressure blocs like the winegrowers and to impose certain necessary reforms even against once omnipotent lobbies. There can be no doubt that one ground for the disillusionment of the average French voter with his rights as a citizen was due to the flagrant contrast between the lavish promises of electoral campaigns and the scandalous failure to keep the promises which resulted from the incoherence of French parliamentary government. General de Gaulle had promised France that it should be governed; it has been. To do this he has had to make many enemies and incur unpopularity, but France has needed a government which was ready to incur unpopularity. To have a first citizen whose greatest virtue and greatest weakness is an indifference to mere popularity is an important piece of political education in a country which has suffered so much from leaders who dared not lead. That the government was prepared to lead was shown by the astonishing boldness with which General de Gaulle grasped the problem of the Empire. He offered all the constituent former colonies the option of leaving the French Community or remaining in it on terms of equality with the metropolis. In what was surely a great demonstration of confidence in France, only one territory left the Community. And the idea and ideal of a French citizenship not confined to France have far more reality when membership in the Community is voluntary than they could have in the not very distant days when all final decisions were made in Paris and when the powers of the colonies were concessions from a kindly but superior mother country. The Community, as it is called in conscious imitation of the British Commonwealth, will not have an easy passage; but it certainly is worlds removed from the old idea of the French Empire.

If it holds together, it will set an example to many new nations which are prone, in the first flush of national freedom, to look askance at even the most reasonable schemes of cooperation with their neighbors or even with their former rulers. If the idea of citizenship in a society united by common ideals and a common culture proves viable, the Community (it does not even insist on the adjective French) will be giving the world a much needed lesson.

But there remains the real thistle, Algeria. It is impossible to say at this moment what is the policy of General de Gaulle or what chances there are of a reasonable and peace-bringing solution. So much blood has been shed, so many crimes committed on each side, that it is hard to be optimistic. But General de Gaulle has continuously insisted on the respect due to the Algerian rebels who are fighting for a concept of dignity which he wishes to preserve. He at least does not talk of Algeria as being simply a part of France or of the loyalties of an Algerian being simply summed up in loyalty to the authorities of the French state. He has promised the investment in Algeria of very great sums of money which, indeed, many Frenchmen feel, though few say, could be more profitably spent in France herself. He has met some of the criticisms of French methods made by the French church. And if the signs of dawn are faint, there are some signs, whereas before there were none.

In another way, the old French idea of the authority of the state and the role of the citizen has been transformed. General de Gaulle was known to friend and foe as an uncompromising nationalist. He was known to be a rigid defender of the idea of French "grandeur." He had opposed and helped to defeat the scheme of a European Defense Community, and it was feared that once in power he would either undo or at any rate prevent the development of such moves toward European integration as had been made. The reality has been very different. To the astonishment and gratification of Europe, General de Gaulle has been the most effective patron of a real rapprochement with Germany, the friend, ally, and, it is believed, mentor of Dr. Adenauer. The high notion he had and has of the dignity of being a Frenchman has not been an obstacle to his practical promotion of the idea of a more and more closely integrated Europe. The "common market" is in existence, and each month that it exists makes the creation of a common European spirit easier. For reasons which I do not understand, there is far less anti-German feeling in France now than there was after the first world war, although there is far more reason for anti-German feeling, considering the horrible experiences of the occupation. The idea of "La France seule" has been abandoned. It is in close collaboration with her neighbors that the future greatness of France is seen to lie. The French idea of the citizen revealed to the world in 1789 had its international as well as its national elements, but for long enough the national completely hid the international aspect. For most Frenchmen, Stephen Decatur was right: it was a case of my country right or wrong. The Algerian war has revealed that many Frenchmen do not hold this simple belief any longer. And the success of the European idea in winning the support of young Frenchmen and the practical achievements of the various European organizations have shown that for many Frenchmen and *perhaps* for most the idea of a citizenship limited in aims and duties to France itself is now seen to be quite inadequate for the world in which France has to live.

CITIZENSHIP IN THE UNITED STATES

THE IDEA AND THE ideal of citizenship have had both in England and in France a long and complicated historical evolution. Of course the same idea in the United States has a long historical ancestry in the Western political tradition and especially in English political tradition. But the United States is unique among the nations of the Western world in having not only a specific birthday (Switzerland and Canada have that), but a birthday followed by what can be called a confirmation ceremony in which the newborn child of 1776 was given, in 1787, a charter of powers and a standard of behavior; and among the political concepts of that charter was the concept of citizenship. Constitutional amendments and judicial interpretation have given to the idea of "a citizen of the United States" a legal concreteness which is not only lacking in the idea of a British subject but is also lacking in the idea of a French citizen, since France has undergone since 1789 so many revolutions and has endured so many contradictory interpretations of the rights and duties of a citizen.

It is not only the fact that the concept of a citizen is basic in the history of the United States, that "We the People" of the Constitution is, at any rate, an expression of the common political purpose of citizens, whether they are conceived of as being isolated in the States or already as being part of a body politic, the United States; there has been also from the beginning a concept and problem of dual citizenship, for the citizen of the United States has also been a citizen of a given state (we can disregard the transitory ambiguities of territorial citizenship), and there has been—and is—a conflict of right and obligation between the citizen of the United States and the citizen of the States which together constitute the Union. It is visible, if from one point of view regrettable, that the whole trend of American history has been to absorb the citizenship of the individual state in the citizenship provided for and defined by the Union. But even the most extravagant doctrine of federal supremacy still did not exhaust the residual right of the States to define both the rights and the obligations of citizenship.

Then, the American governmental system is openly based on the free assent by the consenting citizen to a specific form of government defined by state constitutions and by the Constitution of the United States. It is almost impossible to reduce the British constitution to any legal formula; and France has had too many constitutions since 1789 (I compute sixteen) for any one of them to evoke spontaneous loyalty or any deep hope. But the situation is very different in the United States. As Lord Acton pointed out, by basing all governmental powers on the consent of the governed, by starting afresh in 1776 or in 1787, the American people, or, if you prefer it, the people of the States, opened a new era in history in which political authority was delegated from the bottom up and in which no appeal was made to mere tradition or to the mere authority of the accomplished fact.

There is, of course, an element of fiction in this view of American constitutional law. What the colonists did in asserting their independence was deeply conditioned by history, above all by the history of England. The colonists began by asserting what they claimed to be the rights of Englishmen and, if only because the common law survived, their views of the rights of man were profoundly influenced by English precedent. However, the American then and now is, formally at least, a citizen of two bodies politic based on free choice and based on specific legal documents creating and defining rights and duties. It would be absurdly unrealistic to think that the American, faced with the claims of his nation, reacts in coldly legalistic terms. Nevertheless, the fact that his dual system of government is legalistic and formal and makes no claim to reverence bred by many centuries of political habit does mean that the American attitude to the problems of citizenship differs substantially from the English or the French.

One consequence is that mere reverence for political authority is rare in the United States. There is great, even superstitious, reverence for the Constitution, for the Declaration of Independence, for "the American way of life." But the president apart, the official embodiment of the authority of the United States or the separate States seldom gets the tradi-

tional respect and semi-automatic obedience which
the embodiment can expect and get in England and
more surprisingly gets even in France, where the
habit of obedience to the State has survived so many
bloody disputes about who rightly exercises the
authority of the State.

It is not merely a matter of legal doctrine;
American historical experience has made it difficult
for Americans to revere any given embodiment of
political authority. Even if the American people are
deeply loyal to the American way of political life, the
creation of new states, the astonishing mobility of the
population, the influx until quite recent times of
great masses of immigrants from Europe, have all
combined to make the organization of political consent and political loyalty a continuing problem, not
one to be taken for granted or assumed to have been
solved in the distant past.

Nowhere has the American genius for practical
politics been better displayed than in the handling of
this problem. Contrary to the hopes and expectations of the founding fathers, the United States under
the new Constitution very rapidly developed a national party system, and there can be few intelligent
commentators on the American past and present who
do not see in the national parties one of the great
sources of nationality and one of the practical ways of
creating political obedience in a society so diversified
in climate, racial origin, and local tradition.

Thus sectional loyalties, spontaneously created by
geographical conditions and by local and powerful
traditions, as in New England, have been tamed by

the national party system. Thus the most easily identifiable section, the South, marked off by climate, by its basic economy, by the special character of its population, black and white, has been, except for a brief interval, kept national by the party system. It was not at all accidental that the last national bodies to split before the "War between the States" were the parties, and that the first steps on the "Road to Re-union" were taken by the political parties, specifically by the Democratic party. For these reasons, the parties play a role in organizing and defining citizen-ship and in giving their members an opportunity to fulfil duties and to exercise rights that seem, from a European point of view, extraordinary or even ex-cessive. Few things more surprise a European ob-server of the American political system than the degree to which the internal life of parties is regulated by law. Yet this regulation is indispensable if the parties are to perform their function; and if they do not perform this function, the concept of national citizenship might well be emptied of all real meaning. You cannot, that is to say, separate the idea of the citizen and the idea of the party voter. The totally independent voter, the mugwump, is an essential part of the American picture of citizenship, and many mugwumps are the salt of the earth. But it may be safely said that the United States cannot afford too many mugwumps and that the docile voter who votes the straight ticket is not the idiot of highbrow criticism but the representative American citizen. Thanks to the primary system, he is not in fact quite as docile or as blind or as tradition-ridden as some critics assert. It could be argued (and I should argue it) that the American citizen has in fact a freer choice of representatives and really a more effective voice as far as the personnel of politics is concerned than has his English or French brother. But be that as it may, it is an indisputable fact that the political rights of the American citizen are given to him under a party form.

Then the American citizen as a mere voter or as a party voter is a member of a society in which every form of organization is tolerated or encouraged and in which every form is in competition with every other form. As was noted earlier, this truth struck Tocqueville very forcibly, and, thinking of a France in which nonstate activity was frowned on, he admired, though not quite uncritically, the organizing passion of the American. True, in the England of Tocqueville's time free organization was almost as common and as much a national passion as it was in America; however Tocqueville had not visited England when he made his famous visit to America—if English law and custom were very tolerant of private organizations, English law and custom favored some organizations over others. There was a state church with important formal and some real privileges; there were state institutions professing to establish standards in the arts and sciences; there were hereditary institutions like the House of Lords. There was an undefinable but real social atmosphere in which certain types of societies were superior to others and certain groups in society had prescriptive rights to precedence and respect. In America, not only were

all men equal, but all societies were equal. George
Washington totally failed to induce congress to set up
a national university. John Quincy Adams totally
failed to make the federal government a patron of
learning and science. The puny remnants of church
establishment in New England were being swept
away in Tocqueville's time. New colleges, new
societies, new social phenomena like the lyceum
movement, were all in earnest and sometimes in
bitter competition for the attention, the funds, and
the respect of the average American. And they were
in competition with the persons embodying state
authority. Even more than in England, far more
than in England, the American citizen had his possibilities of action defined for him by private societies.
If it was unrealistic to think of the citizen as exercising his rights apart from the party system, it was
equally unrealistic to think of him as exercising his
rights apart from the churches, the colleges, the societies for promoting this and that, and even the
infant and not very robust trade union movement.
More than that, the great wave of feeling rather than
doctrine which we call the Jacksonian revolution not
only swept away such a centralizing and normative
institution as the Bank of the United States; it also
made political authority more popular but less impressive by the full development of the spoils system,
of rotation in office, and of nearly universal election
to executive and judicial posts. True, the last aspect
of the Jacksonian revolution was confined to the
states. The Constitution, now sacred, saved the
Union from an elected judiciary and from an execu-

tive divided among a number of elected officers. But it was assumed by Jackson (as later by Lenin) that any citizen could carry out any administrative job and that the more citizens who got the chance to do this, the healthier the state of the Republic.

There was perhaps more to be said for this innocent view in a pre-industrial age than there is today. But it is quite obvious that a society based on this optimistic view of the potentialities of the average man was very different from that of France, with its professional bureaucracy, or from that of the mainly amateur government of England based on an unquestioned system of social hierarchy. The American citizen was assumed to be able to do more than the British subject. He was also asked to do more.

For one consequence of the democratic revolution in the United States was to impose on the voter a series of burdens unequalled since the civic life of the old city states. Thus, I believe that the primary system, given the fundamental importance of the party system, was an indispensable reform, especially in a one-party area like the South; but the primary system imposes on the American voter a far greater burden of choice than is imposed on the English or French voter. Whether the election of judges is a good thing or not, it is at any rate in form an additional burden. If the division of the executive power in the state executive among a number of elected officers is a bad thing (I think it is), it is more certainly a burden on the conscientious voter.

When in addition to the mere election of all kinds of public officers from the local dog-catcher to the president of the United States and to the rehearsal of these elections imposed by the primary system there is added in many states the burden of voting on propositions submitted to referendum or on state constitutional amendments, one must have sympathy for the American citizen who, unlike the Athenian citizen, has much more to do than vote and, unlike the Athenian citizen, is not paid for carrying out his political obligations. If it is true, as it is true, that the American does not vote as dutifully as the Englishman or the Frenchman, he has this excuse, that he is asked to vote far more often and is asked to exercise his judgment in ways from which the Englishman and the Frenchman are totally excused. In many states he is in fact asked to do more than even the most public-spirited and enlightened citizen can be expected to do, and by staying away from the polls or blindly voting the straight ticket, he is protesting against excessive demands made on him by the concept of citizenship in the State and in the Union.*

If the American federal system imposed excessive burdens on the citizen and made excessive demands on his virtue and vigilance, until quite recent times it demanded a little more than this political service. Federal taxation was light; federal legislation seldom

* Visiting some friends in San Francisco during a presidential election, I weighed on the bathroom scales the literature issued to the voters to enable them to decide on propositions affecting the county of San Francisco and the state of California. This literature weighed nearly a pound; it was printed in small and bad type and would have involved several days' close study before any citizen could have rationally made up his mind as to what his duty was. In addition, the unfortunate voter had to choose a long range of federal, state, and local officers from the president of the United States down.

affected the man in the street. Nor indeed were the
duties of the good citizen primarily those he owed to
the Union. The reform movements of the late
nineteenth and early twentieth century were primarily state and civic movements. If "turn the
rascals out" was an adequate program for the good
citizen, the rascals were usually in the city hall or in
the state capitol. Local authority was casual and
amateur, and if it was often inefficient, it was not as a
rule burdensome. It was quite natural to think of the
states (as Bryce did) as laboratories of social and
political experiment, and a good citizen might adequately fulfil his political obligations entirely in terms
of his duty as a citizen of a State. The duty of the
federal government was, as Professor Smellie has put
it, the division of an economic dividend. And even
that most burdensome function of the state, heavy in
England and much heavier in France, the burden of
national defense, meant little to the average American. He might never see a warship and might, indeed, seldom see a soldier.

It is one of the truths of comparative politics
which it is always timely to recall, that political habits long survive the conditions which produced and
justified them; and I think it is true that many
Americans, even in 1959, live by the ideas and wish
for the institutions of the period before the world war
of 1914. Some dream of the abolition of the federal
income tax; others, of the reduction of federal functions to what they were before the election of Woodrow Wilson. But there is no chance of getting back
to the days of Wilson and still less to the days of

Jefferson; and the beginning of wisdom for the American citizen today is to realize that his most important duties and his most important rights lie in the sphere of federal government.

There are several reasons for this state of affairs. The integration of the economy begun by the completion of the railroad system, fostered by such federal institutions as the tariff and the Federal Reserve System, would, in any case, have extended federal power and diminished state autonomy. In the age of United States Steel and Standard Oil, the idea of a really sovereign State, master of the economy of its own territory and meeting all the needs of its citizens, was already a dream. But the speed with which federal power and federal burdens were increased owed a great deal to the impact of war. The first world war created a national debt on an unprecedented scale. That alone made the dreams of a merely nominal federal income tax—dreams widely shared in 1913—vain. The necessities of war forced on the federal government the exercise of many powers which might, in other circumstances, have remained those of the States—at any rate, for a decade or so longer. Even the attempt to return to "normalcy" in 1921 was doomed to failure. The decision to go back to a high tariff in a world in which the United States was a creditor, not a debtor, was a decision, for good or ill, affecting the whole of the economy. The decision to commit the federal government to a close control and support of the railroad system was irreversible. The beginning of an elaborate system of grants-in-aid, e.g., for roads,

meant that the citizen began to expect to receive
from the federal government services he had hitherto
demanded from the States. The trust policy of the
federal government, effective or ineffective, impinged
on the whole economy. And although the Supreme
Court oscillated in its decisions about federal economic power, the trend was in favor of the extension of
the powers of the Union. The courts might, for the
moment, reverse congressional legislation on child
labor; but that congress should begin to legislate on
such topics was significant and ominous for the old
idea of States' rights and revolutionary for the
citizen's concept of his relationship to the State and
the Union.

But whatever the possibilities of limiting federal
action were in the post-war boom, they disappeared
in the depression. States became insolvent; cities
became insolvent. The national sickness was truly
national. The policy of relief and redress has to be
national too. The trend is visible even in the last
years of the Hoover administration, and the New
Deal, in this if in nothing else, was truly revolutionary. It undertook to administer a national policy
and to enter spheres of legislation and administration
hitherto left to the States or to private enterprise, the
enterprise of business or the enterprise of charity.
Despite the serious efforts made to enlist the States
as partners of the Union, efforts that were in detail
often successful, power passed irretrievably to the
Union. The citizen, whether he liked it or not, was
now enmeshed in the federal system, and it was not
often that state government mattered as much to him

as federal policies did. He asked for more from the Union; he got more. But the federal government also demanded more. The social security number became not only a proof of the benevolence of the federal government but a mark of its intrusion into the center of the citizen's economic life. And the income tax and the other tax burdens laid by the federal government eclipsed those laid by the states at least as much as federal services eclipsed those offered by the States.

Again, war accelerated a process that was going on in any case. The degree to which the federal government had undertaken to manage the national economy in the first war was immensely increased in the second. That war lasted much longer, distorted the economy of the nation and the way of life of the citizen much more than the first war had done. The citizen got used to being organized and ordered about by the federal government, and even if local men and local authorities were used, as in the case of draft boards, the law they administered and the power they exercised came from Washington. For a great many of the problems that now afflicted the citizen, the only political remedy, if there was one, was in Washington.

For example, it was very largely by federal legislation and federal administration that the trade unions, in 1933 a secondary source of power and a secondary field for the exercise of good or bad citizenship, became organizations of the first order. The unification of the economy tended in any case to bring about a unification of the labor market, but federal legislation (e.g., demonstrated in wages and hours legislation) put the power of the federal government behind this unification and made what had been in law and very largely in fact a local concern of the voter, as far as it was his concern at all, a national interest.

Inevitably, this extension of federal power affected both the theory and the practice of citizenship. If the federal government did not as yet regulate elections in the States, the courts banned some forms of state autonomy, e.g., the white primary. The most enthusiastic defender of States' rights, if he reflected in cold blood on what his voters wanted, knew that in many cases they could get it only by federal action or possibly by federal and state action in collaboration. It was no longer true that the states were effective laboratories for social experiment. The basic and minimum conditions of social action by government authority were laid down by the federal government; and if state government in many places remained healthy and interesting, it was no longer true that states could determine by themselves how much or how little they would do in the general field of social security and social legislation. Hours and wages, pensions and subsidies, were now matters of federal concern. The farmer, dependent on a parity payment, was no more independent of federal action than the worker, enrolled in a union fostered or supported by federal legislation and relying on unemployment payments in part determined by federal policy. If only because the federal government took not only the cream but much of the milk of tax revenue, the old equal balance of dual federalism was fatally disturbed. And peace turned out not to be quite peace. The "cold war" meant both an almost intolerably high level of federal taxation and the perpetuation in peace of military conscription, the exercise of a sovereign power that no State had ever claimed.

And the States themselves, however much they might protest against federal usurpation, were in fact affected by the climate of opinion and by the range of federal action. Few states, even in the fields in which they were still effective, could take a hands-off position. Both as a federal voter and as a state voter, the elector came to expect much more from political action than he had done as late as the beginning of Wilson's first term. He might protest his rugged individualism, but in practice, whether he was a worker whose conditions of employment were regulated by federal legislation or by union power or a great business depending for its most important orders on the Pentagon, there was no escape from the impact of politics. And in such a world the citizen had new duties, new obligations, new rights, for which the traditional doctrines of the fathers provided an inadequate guide.

That those doctrines would be inadequate would not have surprised the founding fathers, some of whom had doubts about the survival of a united republic spread over so great an area. Others had fears for the impact of the outside world on the infant republic, and none would have been surprised at the new stresses and strains imposed on a Union far greater in area than any they had foreseen and far more implicated in the affairs of the outside world than any could have feared. That the traditional liberties of the Americans would be in novel danger in this new world these prudent men would have foreseen—that they could be preserved by a mere blind faithfulness to the customs of the ancestors neither Hamilton nor Madison would have believed for a moment.

That many of the attitudes of the past are now in whole or in part out of date must be plain to the reflective citizen. The material changes and dangers are too obvious for all but the most blind to be able to ignore the need for a recasting of the attitudes of the good citizen, for a reassessment of his duties and opportunities.

What are some of the necessary adjustments that must be made? One is implicit in what I have already said of the new impact of the government, state and federal, on the citizen and on the economy. It was natural and perhaps it was also right to assume in the great days of the makers of "big business" that the businessman was the representative American, the most useful American, the man whose standards and ambitions were those which most Americans should and did admire. There is a great deal to be said for this view, and there was more to be said in the past, when the States and the Union did as little as they did between the end of the Civil War and the beginning of the twentieth century. It was then natural to see politics and politicians as auxiliaries of business, not as equal partners, and still less as masters. Of course, it was a fiction even then to think of business as operating in a vacuum. The world that it transformed was a world defined by law and deeply affected by the policies of the federal if not of the state government, by tariffs, by land policy, by railroad policy, by monetary policy. Business and businessmen did not neglect politics; they used it. Without going to all the dramatic lengths of a conspiracy theory of politics in which presidents and senators appear simply as tools, more or less conscious tools of the "robber barons," it is hard to deny that the relationship of politics and business was an equivocal one, with business both more potent and more prestige-laden.

Despite the prominence given in formal history to the politicians, it is a defensible position that the businessmen were far more important and that the special character of American society in the period of the creation of the new industrial America owed so much to the businessman that an uncritical adulation was legitimate or at any rate pardonable.

But even in that golden age, the role of the political order was basic. The greatest business magnates could not have worked their wonders in a less great and less rich territory than that of the United States. The long immunity from external war, the complete establishment of the authority of the United States as a result of the Civil War—these were political preconditions of the creation of the business empire. So was the American climate of opinion that both rewarded materially on a scale unprecedented in history and gave credit as well as cash, admiration as well as prodigious fortunes. It provided also the necessary auxiliaries, the hundreds of thousands who aided the captains of industry, the millions who were more or less content with the social and political system.

But if it is possible to see business fending for itself up to the first term of Woodrow Wilson, it is hard to see it doing so after the coming of the first world war. No business was as big as the business of war; no business could go its way unaffected by the character of the war and of the peace.

Already, the primordial importance of politics had been insisted on by Theodore Roosevelt. If he did nothing else as president (and of course he did a great deal), he insisted that the government of the United States was not simply another type of corporation, doing business with J. P. Morgan on equal terms. It had a greater power and a greater and nobler responsibility than any corporation, however big, could have.

That this was true ought to have been evident, but it was one of the curious "archaic" features of the twenties that an attempt was made to return, in more than in foreign policy, to simpler days. It was a time when President Coolidge said that "the business of the United States is business"; although he probably did not mean what the public crudely assumed that he meant, his dictum was revealing. It was the age in which Henry Ford I got an adulation that none of his predecessors in the business world had ever known and was, despite his manifest unfitness, seriously talked of for president of the United States.

But that dream world came to an end in 1929, and the basic importance of the political order was brutally insisted on. Perhaps the economy would have recovered by itself in the long run; but as Keynes put it, "in the long run we are all dead," and the American people were not willing to wait for a recovery that not all could be confident they would live to see. Something quicker was wanted, and only government, only the federal government, could provide it. The impact of the new "social service" state has already been dwelt on. What need emphasis here are the direct political results and their impact on the rights and duties of the citizen.

In the first place, there is a neglect of what was the most important service performed by the politicians during this disastrous era of faith shattered and hope daily dwindling. This was the preservation in the mind of the average American of trust in the general benevolence of the American way of life. It might not be giving all that it had promised, but somewhere in the system there was a remedial power. And that power was political.

I do not think that this truth can be effectively denied, yet there is in the American attitude to the politician an ironical admiration that allows for the need for politicians but does not insist on any automatic admiration or formal respect for office holders (the slightly sneering character of the word is itself significant). There are good historical reasons why this should be so, why an American office holder or mere job holder should not have the prestige of an English or French, much less of a German, official.

If Jackson was right that any citizen could fill any job, or nearly any job, there was no place for reverence, and it would be very foolish to expect and indeed undesirable to achieve a general atmosphere of respect for politicians as such.

But if this is so, it does not follow that a casually superior attitude to the function of the politician is equally natural and equally admirable. Yet the belief that the politician, the employee of the State or of the Union, is necessarily a type of American inferior to the go-getter who has "met a payroll" is a dangerously widespread attitude among Americans who regard themselves, with a fair degree of justice, as good citizens. A politician is not thought of as being *serious*, as a businessman or a professional man is. Again, there are historical explanations of this attitude. The spoils system was not likely to produce an official class marked by technical competence. More important, the belief, which once had some justification, that the politician was not performing any fundamental functions justified contempt both for the function and the functionary. If what he did, did not matter very much, it did not matter very much who did it.

The consequences may be, are, serious at more than one level. It may not matter a great deal that rural government in many areas is still unreformed, the province and the perquisite of the "courthouse gang." But as the economy gets more and more integrated, the inefficiency and the archaic character of local government at that level will lead to its atrophy. And a respected system of local government at the grassroots has been basic to the American concept of citizenship. The immediate business of the community *should* be done by those in immediate touch with the people affected. The local community *should* produce the local leaders; but if those local leaders are visibly inadequate for the demands of this age, the grass is poisoned at the roots and the result of the poisoning is the replacement of the county or the town by the State. And it is not *quite* impossible that there may be replacement of the town and the county by some federal office.

The same problem can be found at all levels of the governmental system. The claims of a candidate for office are often enough weighed in very different scales from the claims of an applicant for a private job or the claims of a businessman for leadership in the business community. It should of course be made plain that for many political jobs the rational grounds for election or appointment may not be the same, cannot be the same, as those which are valid in the business world. The candidate whom the critically "good" citizen can vote for with hope and confidence may inspire that hope and that confidence by qualities very different from those of a successful corporation executive. Even in these days of public relations and of the importance attached to the public image of the firm, the place of persuasion is higher in politics than in business. The politician must organize consent and support where a businessman, however politely, is giving orders. And so the politician must be pardoned many tricks of the trade, many examples of bogus geniality, many exhibitions of democratic "friendliness," that a businessman or a professional man has neither the time nor the need for. A bedside manner may be important to a doctor, but it is not so important to its possessor as its equivalent is to a politician, climbing up the ladder of political promotion by organizing support and consent.

A society in which the politician does nothing but organize personal popularity, win personal support, and gain consent for trivial or private issues is not a healthy political society, and voters who tolerate or encourage so mechanical and empty a conception of the democratic process are not good citizens.

It always mattered a bit that mere play actors, mere playboys, could sometimes have their theatrical talents rewarded by high office. There are few regions of the United States (though there are some states like North Carolina) which have not, at some time, succumbed to the temptation to treat political awards as a kind of sport, no more serious than, perhaps not as serious as, college baseball. In the political America of today there are few jobs that the good citizen can afford to treat frivolously, even if only because every job so treated involves the whole political system in some degree of discredit.

It is true that the States are not so effectively autonomous as they were, that forces whose power cannot be evaded reduce their freedom of action. But the States are still political organizations which for good or ill affect the lives of the citizens and often can make or mar the political health of the community. It is therefore unfortunate when so great a representative and so great an executive office as that of governor is won by demagogy or allowed to go by default to some exploiter of frivolous issues treated as part of a game or of grave issues treated as part of a melodrama. It is one of the misfortunes of the segregation issue that it makes the second role so tempting and so profitable, makes the still small voice of reason so hard to hear, and permits the weakening of the prestige and long-term efficacy of the most important state office. The citizen who, under the influence of natural emotion, disregards the long-term price that will have to be paid for the gratification of a short-term resentment may find—or his children may find—that the price is very high.

I am assuming that it is desirable to keep as much life in the state system as possible. In a country the size of the United States, with such varying regional needs and traditions, a failure of state government can only result in the extension of federal bureaucracy. I say federal bureaucracy rather than federal power, since because of the size of the country, federal power could only be exercised bureaucratically. It could not be exercised by and through congress. And whatever technical advantages such a system might bring about (and some state government is so much behind the times that I can conceive of some advantages accruing from a federal assumption of power), the politically disastrous effects would be great indeed. It would mean the overloading of the federal system to a dangerous degree and, what is more to the point in our context, the exclusion of the citizen from a determining voice in many fields of political action that concern him deeply.

But the enemy of the preservation of effective state power and so of the opportunities open to the citizen for service is not only the demagogue, not only the exploiter of an inflammable issue. It is always dangerous to the health of the body politic when the claims to authority are palpably fictitious. And in American state government, there is another deeply embedded weakness that will more and more undermine the moral claims of state government to respect and already has created a class of second-class citizens. It is notorious that in most states the allocation of seats in one house and in some states the allocation of seats in both houses defy the principle of "one man, one vote." That principle is not absolute. There is a case for weighting representation to secure the rights, even the privileges, of groups that might be threatened by a rigorous system of arithmetical allocation of seats. This principle is enshrined in the system of election to the Senate of the United States and, to a lesser degree, in the system of electing the president of the United States. But the presidential election never now distorts the popular will, although alarm is expressed every four years as to what might happen if a few thousand votes in a few selected states were cast this way or that. It is true that the letter and the spirit of the Constitution are both sinned against by the refusal of many states to redistrict, but the House is reasonably representative all the same and the president does embody the choice of the majority of the American people in a way that makes the office a force for national union.

In the States there is no such redress for the inequitable allocation of seats, sometimes reflected in the system of election for governor. It is not a matter of protecting a small minority from the aggression of a majority but of securing the minimum rights of the majority. And as it is the rural counties that gain by this system, and as the most urgent problem of American politics today is to find institutions and habits suitable to an urban society in a technological age, these absurd systems of representation are not only among the chief obstacles to efficient government, but by the obstacles they put in the way of effective political action they serve also to depress the civic spirit of even the most tenacious and the most worthy voters. If the attempts to secure the return from the federal government of alienated powers have come to nothing, if many great interests resist any such transfer and support federal claims, surely one reason is the unrepresentative character of so much state government. A state power based on a rotten borough system is a weak reed to lean on in the war for the preservation of the local basis of American government!

Equally important, in the not very long run, will be the continued evasion of the federal Constitution and of the spirit of American constitutional principles inherent in making the right to vote a matter of race. It would be absurd not to notice that the failure to secure to every American citizen the right to vote on the same terms as his neighbor is a weakness to

America in the cold war. I am more concerned to stress that it is a weakness in the theory and practice of citizenship in the States, as well as a constant temptation and a constant justification of federal intervention. For the arguments that are used today to justify the practical exclusion of the Negro from the ballot in a state like Mississippi prove too much. They deny the democratic premises that men (and women) should have a voice in the making of the laws that they must obey. The implication that one group can be trusted to look after the needs of another ignores not only the fact that they may not know and may not feel the needs but that a third outside party may be, on these terms, a better judge of needs and legitimate feelings than any of the parties immediately concerned. A defense of States' rights based on a denial of equal suffrage is a dangerous weapon indeed for the ideal of local autonomy!

In the same way, the use or the threat of violence, the encouragement of an attitude of inflexible resistance to what has been declared the law of the land, however tempting, is both an example of dangerously bad citizenship and an occasion of it in others. It is hard (as the prohibition experience showed) to pick and choose among the laws that you will consent to obey. Civil order is a seamless web, torn at great risk and hard to repair. The good citizen will have to be very confident of the gravity of the evils he is avoiding—and confident that he can avoid them—before he can, even with a minimum of good conscience, embark on a course of sabotage.

It is difficult to see how the Constitution could

have been made to work, how the presidency could have performed its nationalizing function, how the wounds of the Civil War could even have been partially healed, but for the existence of the national parties. It is easy enough to point out how absurd it is for people of Maine and Texas to vote for the same national ticket for reasons that have nothing to do with current issues but a lot to do with the dramatic and traumatic historical experiences of a century ago. The independent, intelligent, honest elector whom we have been taking as our norm is often baffled when he casts his national ballot for a ticket of which he knows little and helps by his vote to produce a congressional majority whose effective authority will be in the hands of committee chairmen of whom he knows nothing, chairmen who will ignore the party platform on which, formally, the presidential candidate has run. There is nothing to be said for this system except that it does elect presidents who have adequate moral authority; that it does make possible a fairly effective minimum of authority in congress so that some business can be done; and that it has, save in the case of one catastrophe, always succeeded in keeping the people of the United States from asking passionate and profound questions that might wreck the whole system.

Yet the artificial character of the American party system presents problems for the citizen and for the Republic. The existence of "solid" areas, not only the Solid South but the Solid Northeast, has distorted politics, since it has meant the crushing together in the same party structure of voters with widely differing, indeed deeply opposed, points of view, interests, and sentiments. Tempered by the primary system, the one-party states have managed to get along without any finally fatal disasters; indeed, where state politics only are involved, the situation might not deserve much attention. But state politics are involved with national politics, and it is the American citizen who is bewildered, at the national level, by the ambiguous character of the national verdict. It is one thing and a dangerous thing to insist on a rigorously doctrinal party system operating uniformly all over the Union and another to accept without question a party system that has no grounds of unity except historical tradition.

Yet there are signs that the old, purely historical, purely sectional party system is giving way to one more adapted to the needs of modern America. In an age when there are Republican congressmen from the South and when the sole congressman from Vermont is a Democrat, there is no need to despair! More important still, the spread of the modern industrial economy over all of the Union and the consequent spreading of a national way of life make the survival of the old sectional attitudes less likely even if, as far as they still survive, they are still more anachronistic. The car, the truck, the bus, the airplane, all work for a more perfect union. And what is the role of the citizen in this more perfect union?

It is surely to cut himself free from the old automatic allegiances. As long as "talking for Buncombe" pays off, automatically, so long will politicians on the national scene talk local bunkum.

This may seem like a too optimistic picture, but the number of times in contemporary America that there *is* some overwhelming local interest that the politician must and should promote at any cost is small. The habit of considering the federal politician simply as a local agent is, in many cases, a traditional survival that has not any very deep roots even in material interest. To send and keep on sending a man back to Washington because he serves local interests with blind fidelity and never lifts his eyes, or his nose, from the claims of his district is to abdicate the responsibility of a citizen in a world where the efficiency and prestige of the American governmental system is an important item in the world's balance sheet. Every congressman or senator who abdicates his national and international responsibilities or who thinks he has adequately met them when he has sounded off, deploring the wickedness of some or all foreigners, weakens the United States and the free world—and represents his voters, as citizens, in a historically defensible but practically dangerous way.

This is not to assert that the voter should pay no attention to local issues. I have already suggested that in state and local politics, he ought to pay more, be more selective, more ready to provide the conditions under which alone local government can flourish. More than that, the solution or nonsolution of local problems not only affects the total health of the United States but affects its position in world opinion. A good PTA is an asset, as is a good hospital system or a good library system. The rising tide of youthful violence is not confined to the United States; it is painfully visible in England and is beginning to appear in France. But the United States is the great exemplar, and failures there are heard 'round the world. I do not know, I do not think anybody knows, the answer to this problem. Better housing, better schools, more effective youth work by the churches— all are remedies even if they are only palliatives. It has even been boldly suggested that more early teaching of the differences between right and wrong, the ending of an ethically neutral system of education, might be part of the answer. But no one can be content with a system in which future citizens—not all of them, by any means, underprivileged—so often show an automatic reliance on violence. And in a society so threatened and so plagued, the seamless web of public order is torn, for whatever motive, at a very great risk. The political education that the future voter receives at home and the degree to which the boy or girl is encouraged to be law-abiding or to express his passions—if you like, his most sacred feelings—in violence are basic to the problem of effective citizenship in the modern world. For we cannot do without citizens; citizenship is not a concept that can be usefully considered apart from the human beings who meet or fail to meet the needs of the free society.

And it is possible, it is perhaps more than possible, that the family throws too much responsibility onto the state and even too much onto the churches and other voluntary organizations. We have visibly a lot to learn about the problems of living in the new industrial world. We can only attain the beginning of wisdom if we realize the degree to which we are moving in a world of unknowns. In that world we should be foolish to abandon too easily what has proved useful in the past or, on the other hand, assume that we can live entirely by the precepts and traditions of a society that is being changed at a revolutionary degree of speed under our eyes. Perhaps we cannot better the Pauline advice to "prove all things; hold fast that which is good."

There remains one last duty of the citizen and of his political representative, his duty, the duty of all Americans to the world. One of the most remarkable and encouraging features of the modern world has been the readiness of the American people to recognize and accept duties outside their own boundaries. Looking back at the troubled years since 1945 when the American people learned that the most complete military victory did not necessarily bring peace, bearing in mind the long hold of isolationism on the American mind, especially in the mind of the American as voter and as elected person, one is entitled to be both surprised and deeply impressed by the acceptance by the American people of the new role history has imposed on them.

It is easy enough to show—and it is often a comforting exercise for a European to indulge in—that in being generous in money and goods, in undertaking new burdens and new obligations not enumerated in the bond of the United Nations, the American people have been pursuing their own enlightened self-interest. They have, but how many nations are always capable of pursuing their self-interest or seeing it or having enough self-control to postpone immediate gains to long-term aims? Certainly in the past, the American people, like the British or the French, have not always shown this selfish minimum wisdom, to their own loss and to that of the world.

That Americans have done so now should be a matter for unreserved rejoicing. But it is my conviction that they have done more than that, that had they been concerned only with their self-interest they would not have seen it so clearly. There has been among the motives for American international good citizenship much more than a prudential desire to restore the world to health, since a sick world is dangerous, more than a desire to find and keep militarily useful allies. There has been what the Quakers call a "concern," a belief that the American people should not pass by the wayside. No doubt the thought that the Soviet Union might turn up performing the role of the Good Samaritan to some degree influenced Americans, but they were more moved by the tradition that insisted that they *should* be Good Samaritans. And they were also moved, I believe, by a feeling, possibly justified, that in the aftermath of the first world war they had not lived up to their own highest ideals or highest wisdom.

Be that as it may, in the United States of today they are few among the citizen body who deny all responsibility for events in the outside world or simply pass by the victims or potential victims whom the world provides in such embarrassing quantities. (It is perhaps worth noting that some of the most verbally vehement enemies of communism in the United

States are indifferent to measures taken to halt it outside the United States.) Despite outbursts by bodies like the Daughters of the American Revolution, there is a widespread acceptance of the fact that a citizen's duties do not stop at the high-water mark. In *some* way, the American citizen today has extranational duties. One of these, of course, has been alluded to. If the American citizen is also a citizen of the world, he has a duty to keep his own house in order, perhaps to give it newer and more "contemporary" furniture. Only so can the United States teach by example the fundamental truths on which the nation is based. And it has been suggested that in the choice of federal spokesmen, the citizen as voter should bear in mind that more is now needed than the most faithful application to the needs of a congressional district or even of a state.

But there is a further problem, not solved by the American voter setting his local political house in order. Measures as well as men are needed, policies as well as honest and broad-minded executants of them. And here the duty of the good citizen is patience. This is an un-American virtue, but one that is deeply necessary. The story of the United States (except for the catastrophe of the Civil War) has been a success story. And it is natural for the American voter, ready to vote money in the billions, ready to accept the draft, ready, if with deep reluctance and resentment, to accept the burden of the Korean war as an international, not a merely national, cause, to want quick results. It is natural but dangerous.

It is dangerous, for the voter may be tempted to succumb to a new form of demagogy, to accept recipes for quick success or to despair if quick success cannot be promised. He will be tempted to support politicians who demand that the noncommitted nations "speak up in meeting" or "stand up and be counted." For the very moral candor and passion that, more than self-interest, have made the American people ready to bear the great burdens imposed since 1945 have their dangers. It may not be wrong to see the outside world in black and white, but it is wrong to expect the outside world to see itself in black and white. It is wrong, that is to say, to expect the outside world, even the most friendly parts of it, to accept American leadership automatically or to see all questions in an American light. The moral fervor which Americans bring to political principles (as apart from their often excessively tolerant attitude to political practices) may have its roots in the Evangelical tradition. The errant nations should accept conversion and testify to it in word and deed. They, alas, will seldom do so, and not often enough for the United States safely to build a policy on it.

If this diagnosis be true, then patience is the most important virtue the American citizen can display (after a conviction that he has a duty to the outside world). For if he does not display it, he will be unjust to his leaders, to the president, to the secretary of state, to his senator and congressmen, who may well have learned in Washington that things are more complicated than they seem to be at home. The domestic virtues of wanting quick results, of disliking secrecy, of insisting on (and too often settling for) the acceptance of grand moral principles, are less visibly virtues on the international scene. There, very imperfect solutions are all that can be hoped for, and the pursuit of perfection can—and usually will—end in deception and disillusion.

And disillusion is one of the great dangers facing the citizen and weakening the effectiveness of the politician. Perhaps, in the past it did not matter that the politician offered a new heaven and a new earth. No one really believed him. In any event, the real business was being done by businessmen. But the real business of the world and of the United States is today being done by politicians (who may in some cases have been businessmen). Just as it is wrong to expect pure or mere business methods to be adequate for the purposes of the political world, it is wrong to expect even American politics, much less American business, to be exportable to a market willing to operate on American lines.

The American citizen as a world citizen will have to be content with small successes, with successes to be hoped for rather than successes immediately realizable. He will have to learn to put up with bad manners, ingratitude, incompetence. And, of course, not all of his political agents will be wise, upright, or lucky. The virtue of patience does not exclude the duty of realistic criticism and of democratic scepticism. Many, but not all, good American political habits will be usable in the outside world. But the failure of the outside world to meet American standards will not absolve the American citizen of his duty to that outside world or make it any less true that a concept of citizenship that does not extend beyond the frontiers of the United States is sterile and self-defeating today. Of course, this truth is not only for the Americans but for the British, for the French, for the citizens of old and new nations, still earthbound by dangerously exclusive national or doctrinal coils at the very moment that man is about to take off into space.